THE PRACTICAL NEGOTIATOR

The Practical Negotiator

I. WILLIAM ZARTMAN
AND
MAUREEN R. BERMAN

New Haven and London
Yale University Press

Published with the assistance of the
A. Whitney Griswold Publication Fund.

Designed by James J. Johnson
and set in Melior type.
Printed in the United States of America by
Halliday Lithograph, West Hanover, Mass.

Library of Congress Cataloging in Publication Data
Zartman, I. William
    The practical negotiator.
    Bibliography: p.
    Includes index.
    1. Diplomatic negotiations in international dis-
putes. 2. Diplomacy. 3. Negotiation.
I. Berman, Maureen R., 1948–   II. Title.
JX4473.Z37   327.2   81-40435
ISBN 0–300–02523–8   AACR2
ISBN 0–300–03097–5

10 9 8 7 6 5 4 3 2

Contents

Foreword

The related problems of settling disputes peacefully before they lead to blows and of bringing about an end to war have occupied statesmen since the days of Nineveh and Tyre. Although religious leaders, moralists, and diplomats began centuries ago to seek ways to promote peaceful settlement, and students like Machiavelli and De Callières put forth their views, the need for study and action was recognized by only a limited number of people before the end of the nineteenth century.

Despite efforts such as the Hague Conferences of 1899 and 1905 and the creation of the League of Nations, it was not until the second quarter of the twentieth century that scholars began to analyze the nature of the complicated relationships among states and to ask why at some times the olive branch is successful and at others the sword prevails. Only very recently have scholars begun to pay serious attention to such questions as: By what process do parties resolve their differences before taking up arms? What factors account for the success of this process? If they fail—or no attempt is made to solve differences peacefully—by what process do parties seek to resolve their differences once fighting has erupted? What role does the individual play in conflict resolution? As in other endeavors, are there some who are especially talented in seeking ways to end disputes? Do some individuals possess natural gifts, or have they learned their craft through apprenticeship or at the bargaining table?

If differences between states are bound to arise, and if there is a brewing or potential threat of the use of force, and if devastation, even world devastation, threatens, can mankind *by taking thought* reduce or even eliminate the danger? Are conflict and dispute settlement susceptible to scientific research that may lead to peace for the world?

These are some of the questions that led to a program now known as Communication and Conflict. Out of a conversation I had in 1968 with Dr. John Schweppe, a distinguished medical researcher and teacher, grew a ten-year program to examine the processes of conflict resolution. As a scientist, Dr. Schweppe proposed that some of the methods of scientific inquiry be applied to a study of the processes of dispute resolution. By so doing, he thought, it might be possible to shed light on the process and thus suggest answers to some of the questions posed above. Dr. Schweppe made a grant to the Academy for Educational Development to start the program and continued supporting it for ten years.

The program's first step revealed two situations quite unlike those in the medical field: one was a yawning gap between researchers and practitioners; the other was the diversity, ranging from philosophy to language, that existed among researchers. The existence of these gaps led to an early decision to interview practitioners to get their views down on paper. It also led to an effort to find out what kinds of research and activities were going on.

Much of the subsequent program has been focused on the gap between researchers and practitioners and the need to make efforts to narrow it. The gap was compounded of ignorance and suspicion. Practitioners tended to resist learning about—even more implementing—the theories of researchers. Many of the theories seemed obscure and totally irrelevant to the practical needs of individuals at the bargaining table. Those findings of scholars that did not seem irrelevant often appeared obvious to experienced practitioners.

As practitioners played down the possible contributions of scholars, so did researchers overlook a valuable resource for information about how negotiations are successfully conducted. Although many skilled negotiators view their work more as an art or craft than as a systematic body of propositions, knowledge, and teachable skills, nevertheless, if skillfully drawn out, they can provide certain lessons.

An initial program focus—one that remained constant throughout—was an attempt to draw out experienced negotiators who were available to talk about the process of negotiation, with particular emphasis on the factors they considered most crucial. The overall question was, "What do you now know about negotiation that you wish you had known at the beginning of your career?"

The first interviews conducted were wide-ranging and touched on a broad array of factors. One of the first interviews was conducted by the director of the program with W. Averell Harriman, whose diplomatic experience has extended over five decades. The interview, which resulted in more than 300 pages of transcript, helped shape the research agenda.

An advisory panel was put together composed largely of experienced international negotiators but including two accomplished labor mediators. At the same time, the Academy entered into an agreement with the Oral History Project at Columbia University to ensure that interviews undertaken would be available to scholars and future negotiators.

The initial interviews showed that systematic inquiry would be facilitated if future interviews were based on a structured questionnaire. With support from the Lilly Endowment, this questionnaire was administered to twenty-five experienced negotiators. To widen the research base, distinguished non-Americans were added to the list of those interviewed.

In 1971 a suggestion was made that a good deal might be learned if it were possible to interview all the participants in one negotiation. This led to the study of the Trieste negotiations of 1954. It had been an unusual situation in that the final stages of the negotiations were in the hands of only five individuals from four nations who, twenty years later, were alive and ready to talk. The interviews were put together in a volume with an introduction by an outstanding student of Balkan affairs, John C. Campbell (Campbell 1976). The volume presents not a detailed history but unscreened and unadulterated recollections and evaluations of the five experienced and skillful individuals who conducted the negotiations. From these recollections it seemed possible to extrapolate factors that might have wider applicability.

At an early stage—and while the interviews continued—the program began focusing on scholarly research that would be of value to practitioners. The first effort in this direction was to give project support to Leonard Doob and William Foltz of Yale University, who had devised a technique of applying psychological research about negotiators to real-life conflict resolution. A problem-solving workshop on the conflict in the Horn of Africa was held in a hotel in the South Tyrol of Italy and brought together unofficial but representative persons of the parties involved—Kenya, Ethiopia, and Somalia (Doob 1970).

Daniel Druckman, a social psychologist, was asked to prepare a volume pulling together the most useful theories of social psychologists who had studied various elements of the negotiating process in a variety of contexts (Druckman 1973).

To facilitate communication between scholars and practitioners, two conferences were organized—one in Greenwich, Connecticut, in 1971 and the other in Bellagio, Italy, in 1973. Both conferences comprised "pure scholars," practitioners, and a few "half-breeds." The wide-ranging agenda specifically included ways to address and lessen the gap that divided the two groups.

The Bellagio Conference, supported by the Charles F. Kettering Foundation and the Rockefeller Foundation and held at the latter's Villa Serbelloni, included an exercise devised to indicate the nature of the gap. Lincoln Bloomfield of the Massachusetts Institute of Technology, an expert in the use of political games, worked out a game the principal purpose of which was to delineate some of the differences between the requirements of the scholar and of the diplomat.

Divided into two groups—scholars and practitioners—the participants were presented with a hypothetical conflict situation or scenario. The practitioners were asked to focus on the essential information or data they would require from scholars, while the scholars were asked to consider the relevance of various theories to understanding practical problems in real life. "Even if practitioners feel the need for additional help," Bloomfield concluded, "they do not know enough about even the categories and conceptual frameworks of social scientists to know what questions to ask" (Berman and Johnson 1977, p. 234). The scholars, for their part, had difficulty generating appropriate responses to the scenario guidelines. Several scholars described their assignment as "an impossible task": "Theories seemed abstract without 'solid grounding in the situation' and 'we would come out looking ridiculous before people who knew a lot more [about facts and realities]'" (Ibid., p. 235).

These comments underlined sharply the need for improved scholar–practitioner communication. Scholars who studied negotiations without consulting or at least attempting to take into consideration the real-life experiences of seasoned practitioners risked two things: failure to capture the essence of the process as it is actually practiced and consequent inability to communicate with negotiators because they failed to understand the process as negotiators perceived it.

Particularly as the number of empirical studies of social psychologists grow in number, the need becomes more pressing to find a way to translate the theoretical findings of scholars into language that practitioners understand and then to test the findings of the laboratory against the experience of practitioners. The Bellagio experiment added impetus to the bridge-building efforts.

By 1975, the program's resources had grown to include: a large body of interviews with experienced negotiators; a record of one important and difficult negotiation provided by the five principal participants; the results of two conferences (one international) at which scholars and practitioners met and discussed areas of research in negotiation, gaps that needed to be filled, and ways in which the two groups could be brought together to make a more effective contribution to each other; and a study of research and experimentation on social psychological aspects of international negotiations.

It was now possible to move on to another stage of the program—refinement of the material collected into a book, primarily for the use of negotiators but of interest to scholars as well, that would analyze the process of negotiation and how best to negotiate. The volume would seek to bridge the gap between social scientists who study bargaining and practitioners who have actual responsibility for carrying out the process. The Rockefeller Foundation agreed to provide added support for this effort, and I. William Zartman, a recognized scholar in the field of international negotiations and diplomatic problems, was enlisted to undertake the work with the cooperation of Maureen R. Berman, then associate director of the Communication and Conflict Program. Dr.

Zartman's knowledge of the scholarly world and his acquaintance with the diplomatic community were important ingredients.

The present volume demonstrates that there is indeed a body of knowledge about negotiation that removes it from the "seat-of-the-pants" category and that tentative conclusions drawn from the experience of the past can be of immense value in a world in which negotiation must become increasingly important.

It is doubtful whether any effort to study the complex subject of negotiation could reach a true culmination at the present time. I believe, however, that Zartman and Berman have carried analysis of the negotiation process a step forward and have shown that the experiences of negotiators fit into a pattern. This volume should both help to narrow the gaps noted earlier and be of great utility to those whose skill in negotiation could significantly affect the difference between success and failure.

If John Schweppe's and my hopes have not been fully realized, at least we can feel that this volume carries one step further the continuing effort to improve mankind's ability to resolve major differences.

Alvin C. Eurich
Academy for Educational Development

We are grateful for the support and continuing guidance of Edward W. Barrett and the research assistance of Robert J. Janosik and Marc M. Wall.

We would like to dedicate this work to Joseph E. Johnson, practical negotiator.

I. W. Z. and M. R. B.

1

Theoretical and Practical Negotiations

A leading figure of both Democratic and Republican administrations in Washington in the 1970s, several times cabinet member and then special ambassador, recounts his annoyance with journalists who attributed his successive cabinet appointments to his skill as a "manager." "I never thought of myself as a 'manager,'" Elliot Richardson explains. "I simply tried to do a good job. But I suspect now they will be writing about my appointments from now on in terms of my experience as a 'negotiator.' Perhaps some day I will find out what that is."

Even such a skilled negotiator suggested by this remark that he felt that negotiation was merely "trying to do a good job." This idea is widespread among diplomats, many of whom believe that if negotiation does require some special skills these come through an acquired "feel of things" and are beyond capture and transmission as rules and theories. This book comes out of an equally time-honored tradition but is built on the opposite assumption. It is a book on negotiation, particularly international negotiation, defined as a process in which divergent values are combined into an agreed decision, and it is based on the idea that there are appropriate stages, sequences, behaviors, and tactics that

1

can be identified and used to improve the conduct of negotiations and better the chances of success.

Studies have been based on this assumption ever since Thucydides first considered Pericles' speech and the Spartan debates worth recording, or, earlier, since Abraham's attempt to bargain with the Lord was deemed worthy of preservation in Scripture. More explicitly, writers in previous ages of great diplomatic activity—notably the seventeenth and eighteenth centuries and the interwar period of the twentieth century—attempted to capture the essence of negotiation in order to pass it on to future practitioners. Their purpose was more than entertainment. They did not want simply to record the feats of great and famous statesmen so that others might admire them, but they hoped rather to transmit an understanding of their strengths and weaknesses so that others might do better.

These were the explicit reasons for the treatises of François De Callières (1716) and his rival and critic Antoine Pecquet (1737), and the same goals generally inspired Sir Harold Nicolson (1964). It is hard to judge their success. Their insights are generally recognized as accurate and still applicable today, and yet each wrote to warn against the coming of an age when diplomacy and negotiation would no longer be held in high esteem or practiced according to the time-honored rules and principles they had recorded. What have we learned since then about the process that can justify yet another attempt to tell negotiators how to negotiate?

NEW EVIDENCE

There are three types of new evidence that permit a new try. The simplest is the historical record. In the more than thirty years since the Second World War, a large number of negotiations have been undertaken with varying degrees of success. Many of them have been reported by political historians, recounted in the memoirs of practitioners, and examined in case studies. In nearly every instance the writers have tried to find the answer to the question, "Why did things turn out the way they did?" From case to case the attempt to explain outcomes is based on the very different factors of the moment, but at least processes and conclusions-as-hypotheses are explicitly treated.

So active has the post–World War II period been that many writers refer to it, as others did to specific earlier periods, as an age of negotiations. The durability and growth in the activities of the United Nations, the explosion in the number of sovereign states in contact with each other, the legal fiction of sovereign equality and the political reality of unequal power, the creation of new international organizations and frameworks, the search for new political and economic world orders, and the vastly expanded number of subjects within the purview of the international community are among the many reasons for the expansion of negotiation in the second half of the twentieth century.

The characteristics of many of the new subjects of negotiation may also affect the nature of the negotiations themselves, so that it is at least conceivable that postwar negotiations differ from earlier ones in significant ways. Negotiations at the height of the cold war gave rise to a spate of writings on negotiating with the Russians, most of which suggested that negotiations with the Russians—and eventually other Communist countries like China and North Korea—were significantly different from negotiations with other peoples. That period may now be past, and the lessons of more recent negotiations, of which there are already many, appear to be more applicable to negotiating behavior in the near future.

A number of postwar cases have been examined in preparing this study, among them: the Trieste negotiations (1954); negotiations over military bases between the United

States and Spain (1963–70), the Philippines (1976), and Morocco (1957–59); British negotiations with Malta over military bases (1971–72); postcolonial negotiations between the former metropoles and Kenya (1963–73), Algeria (1962–65), and Indochina (1954); the Paris negotiations on the Vietnam war (1968–70); Korean armistice negotiations (1950–53); the negotiations over the neutralization of Laos (1960–62); the Panama Canal negotiations (1975–78); the Test-Ban Treaty of 1963, the Eighteen-Nation Disarmament Talks, and the Nonproliferation Treaty; the Strategic Arms Limitation Talks (SALT) I, Interim, and II; the Law of the Sea conferences beginning in 1967; various negotiations between African (and then also Caribbean and Pacific) nations and the European Communities for association status (1961–79); the three disengagement agreements and the cease-fire agreement discussions after the October 1973 war in the Middle East; negotiations to end the Biafran war (1968–69); negotiations from 1977 to 1980 between Egypt and Israel, both before and after President Sadat's visit to Jerusalem in November 1977; General Agreements on Tariffs and Trade (GATT) negotiations; the range of negotiations between the developing and developed nations known generally as the "North-South Dialogue," especially in 1974–75; the Chinese-Vietnamese talks following their seventeen-day war in February 1979; negotiations between the United States and Iran after the invasion of the American Embassy in November 1979 until the abortive rescue attempt in April 1980; and negotiations over the transition to majority rule in Zimbabwe and Namibia between 1976 and 1980.

A second type of new evidence—a dimension perceived only in recent years—comes from more scientific studies that test new and earlier notions about human attitudes in negotiating situations. Since 1960 a large number of research reports—a thousand by one (incomplete) count—have been published by psychologists, sociologists, political scientists, and economists on theories and experiments in bargaining behavior.

This work has generally avoided and often disdained historical studies, considering them discrete, anecdotal, idiosyncratic, and atheoretical. It has led to the construction of a body of theory and a congeries of experimental results that historians and practitioners usually find artificial, irrelevant, contrived, and jargonistic. As Alvin Eurich noted in his foreword to this volume, there have been few attempts to build bridges between the two collections of data or the two groups of scholars. Furthermore, the two types of studies and their authors are mutually unintelligible and therefore cannot be compared without some translation, since the authors speak different languages, explain in different terms, work from different assumptions (including comparability itself), and seek different kinds of answers. When social scientists address themselves to specific cases, they are frequently more interested in testing their theories than in explaining the outcome of a particular negotiation. The more rigorously scientific the theory, the more often it seems simplistic and deterministic to the practitioner.

After all this, one might well wonder about the value or applicability of this new type of evidence, and yet the proper conclusion is that much of it needs to be translated rather than dismissed. Theoretical explanations concentrate on particular terms of analysis, such as learning rates, the number of negotiating parties, or the role of threat in negotiation. These need to be joined to other explanatory variables or parameters in examining particular cases. Some experimental tests focus on effects more significant to the discipline or to theory than to the understanding of a historic case. These need to be separated from experiments that do test recognizable phenomena and therefore lead to a better understanding of negotiation as practiced. Analytical concepts have to be identified in specific cases, so that the real effect can be recognized through its conceptual name. For example, game matrix and utility-curve models conceptualize negotiations as a process of strategic choice and value maximization. But in the history of international negotiations it sometimes becomes difficult to locate such concepts in the diplomats' practice. The process of persuasion and communication may be indirect and implicit in a range of contracts between parties, so that the process of choice and movement is, in reality, broader and looser than the theories imply.

When all this is said, it is still evident that extremely helpful lessons from experiment and theory can be brought to bear on the understanding and even the formation of practitioners' behavior. The lessons can be real if the promise of theoretical study as well as its current limitations are recognized by theoretician and practitioner alike. There is now no theory of negotiation that can encompass and explain the entire process, but there are a number of well-developed theoretical approaches that both open the way for and require much more testing and debate. Theories and experiments from a number of such approaches have been drawn upon, relating to timing, trust, concession rates, threats, side payments, perception, justice, communication, and learning, among others. Few proponents would claim that any of these approaches holds the key to the process, although it would be said of many that they give necessary if not sufficient insights into the determination of outcomes. The entire process combines them all, in ways that may not be theoretically comprehensible, but the parts can be examined for a better understanding of the whole.

A third source of new data is two sets of interviews undertaken specifically for this study. The goal of both interview series was to draw upon the experience and wisdom of persons who have been actively engaged in international negotiations. Indeed, many of those interviewed were participants in the postwar negotiations used as case material. One set of interviews was based on a questionnaire addressed to senior negotiators from the American diplomatic service and from key negotiating positions in other countries.* Their views were sought about aspects of the negotiating process as they had participated in it; as seasoned negotiators they were asked, "What do you know now about negotiations that you wish you had known when you first started?" Out of these extensive interviews came opinions on a wide range of topics such as instructions, tactics, personal and cultural characteristics of negotiators they had dealt with, techniques, summitry, and many other subjects. The interviews also produced a number of anecdotes illustrative of many aspects of negotiations from the insiders' vantage point that complemented the historical record of case studies. The results were inductively useful and, unlike the historical accounts that they resembled, the information was gathered in response to an ordered series of questions on specific topics.

The other set of interviews was based on a different kind of questionnaire addressed to fifty United Nations ambassadors and high members of the U.N. Secretariat.† The interview used mini-scenarios which involved the participant in a simulated negotiating experience. The scenarios were constructed to translate leading hypotheses about the negotiating process into terms easily assimilable by practitioners.

The mini-scenario interviews yielded both confirmations of certain effects and results contrary to others and in the process suggested new hypotheses. The deductive exercise

---

*A list of these interviews is contained in Appendix Part A, and the reader is directed to these interviews throughout the book.
†Appendix Part B.

differed from the results of all previous experiments in that the subjects were seasoned negotiators, rather than random subjects with no experience in practice.

These three types of new evidence are used here to support a study that seeks to be conceptual but not theoretical, realistic but not historical, and useful both to practitioners and theorists.

The result is a paradox. The book tries both to describe and to prescribe; it is a study of what has been done in order to tell both what will and therefore what should be done. It describes and analyzes past practice in order both to foresee and to improve future practice. Yet the paradox is only apparent. The book seeks to identify what is "good" in the best of past practice in order that future negotiations may be better, that is, that both sides may more satisfactorily and more creatively arrive at the joint decision resolving their differences and preserving their interests.

For this to be possible, the art of negotiating must be something that can be learned from books, a point that negotiators have long tended to question. To some extent they are right, of course: One can no more read a book and then win a diplomatic round than one can read a manual and win a tennis match, build a bridge, or paint a masterpiece. Experience is still the best teacher. But in negotiating as in any other field of endeavor, one can prepare, facilitate, and advance the lessons of on-the-job training by analysis of the subject and education on how to handle it. There is nothing that justifies the notion that negotiation is different from any other activity in this respect.

By the same token, book learning can be more or less effective. Its usefulness is maximized if it clearly portrays the essential nature of the subject, using both historical and experimental evidence as this work tries to do, and if this message is presented in a way most assimilable by its intended audience. It is for this reason that so many historical examples are given in the subsequent discussion—not merely to support and illustrate the point but also to present it in a different language, using cases to convey concepts. Diplomats, as avid readers of history and biography, are likely to be more receptive to concrete examples than to hypothetical constructs alone. Optimally, this sort of reading and teaching should then be reinforced by the kind of experience that makes new perceptions and attitudes part of behavior. Herein lies the value of simulation, or of direct application in the real world, although both are outside the scope of this book. Yet beneath an effective learning from history, games, and experience lies a conceptual grasp of the subject that can be taught only on the basis of explicit terms and analysis.

NEW UNDERSTANDING

The study's other innovation, besides a selective use of the past, is the introduction of a particular model to clarify the nature of the process of negotiation. The model identifies three stages in the process and associates different types of problems and behaviors with each stage: (1) diagnose the situation and decide to try negotiations; (2) negotiate a formula or common definition of the conflict in terms amenable to a solution; and (3) negotiate the details to implement the formula on precise points of dispute. The nature of the model and its implications will be elaborated in the following chapters. It will be emphasized—but bears underlining at the outset—that the notion of stages or phases of a negotiation is an analytical one that, while corresponding to reality, is far sharper in concept than is ever the case in human events. In analysis, for purposes of identification and discussion, phases can be isolated and examined in detail, but in the real world they tend to have shady borders, overlap each other, and even hide when their names are called. A boundary problem is always present in the use of concepts. Indeed, it is inherent in many everyday abstractions, such as love, the ages of man, clouds, war and peace, and social drinking. People learn to live with the boundary problem of these concepts, so it should not stand in the way of understanding the negotiation process.

It might be objected that a single model of the process is Procrustean. Might there not be a hundred ways to negotiate, with the one presented here being only one among many? Or worse, might it be merely an American or a Western one among many, with other cultures preferring to do things differently and just as well? Might it not be safer just to stick to checklists, variables, and proverbs, as so many other works have done, without venturing into the more restrictive notion of process sequences?

To the extent that it is accurate, a process model is more useful in ordering and preparing for reality than a mere checklist. Yet the model here is not a rigid construct. It is not just one of many ways to arrive at an agreement, but rather the general path or sequence through which those different ways flow. There may be a number of air routes to Boston, but they all involve the phases of takeoff, cruising, and landing, and in that order! Behavior appropriate to one phase is not necessarily appropriate to another. Apparently different ways of arriving, as well as checklists and proverbs, can find their place within this general understanding of the process. Seen in this analogy the question of ethnocentrism is inapplicable, but that may be dismissing the question too rapidly and without a hearing. The matter of cultural behavior will be examined in the last chapter, but it should be noted here that some interpreters see a major cultural difference in the order in which different negotiators follow the phases of the model. There is not enough evidence to discount this observation and so it will be discussed in more detail below. Suffice it to say here, that part of the present argument is that there is a particular process sequence which, when followed, gives the best results.

Although this study is designed to suggest the way to go about negotiating, it has some important limitations. It cannot tell anyone how to win. In fact, a theoretical understanding of the subject is important because it shows that it is impossible to tell anyone how to do best; one can only learn how to do better. This is true for three reasons inherent in the nature of the process. First, negotiation is a symmetrical process. Every piece of advice that is available to one party is available to the other, every tactic is open to one as well as the other, both parties can play it tough and come to no agreement or play it soft and give in on crucial points. If one could figure out when the last minute was, one could make an offer one second before the deadline that was minimally acceptable to the other side and too late to be rejected, thereby deciding the terms of the agreement. But if one side had this information—by any other way than by luck and by feel—the other side could have it too. Indeed, if both sides play such strategies as if they were unilaterally available, deadlock is sure to result.

Second, negotiation is not a finite process. Moves can go in all directions, including backtracking. As long as either side can stop or change direction, it is not possible to provide a deterministic theory or winning strategy for the process. Furthermore, the positions, stakes, issues, demands, and minimums of the parties are not all known, and even when "known" are not fixed. Indeed, the essence of the process is to juggle, combine, eliminate, and change any of these elements, and this may involve changing one's own values as well as those of the party or parties. There can be more and less effective ways of doing this, but the indeterminate nature of the ingredients keeps one from setting forth any theory that aspires to be determinate or any strategic recipe that is guaranteed to win.

Third, the participants in a negotiation both anticipate and react, so they have a double motivation. One may well react to one's own or the other party's previous moves, but there is no guarantee that either party will continue to react in the same way. When, instead, a party begins anticipating the other party's reactions, a process of indeterminate regression begins, one that can suggest very different behaviors, depending on when the process stops. Some scholars appear to have developed good theories about how to minimize losses under those conditions, human nature being what it is, but minimizing losses is not the same thing as winning.

Yet despite the limitations of theories and strategies of negotiating, it is necessary for a negotiator to be aware of them, since he must assume that the other party is too (explicitly or intuitively). Prescriptions on negotiating behavior can help any party do better, that is, conduct his business on a higher level of awareness of both substance and procedure, and create the largest possible total sum of benefits out of which each party can get the most.

There are three basic concepts in recent studies that capture well the essence of the negotiation process as one of doing better, not one of winning. One is the game theory notion of "non-zero-sum encounters." The core of the negotiation process is the transformation of zero-sum situations and attitudes into positive-sum solutions and approaches. In the zero-sum situation, one man's loss is the other man's gain, and the process involves one party's taking something from the other. For example, two nations may dispute the ownership of a piece of territory that forms a border between them. Viewed as a zero-sum situation, one of the two nations will be the beneficiary of the land while the other will be left empty-handed. Those who view negotiation in this light can be excused for avoiding it or causing the opponent to shun it.

Zero-sum perceptions are characteristic of a conflict before it becomes the subject of negotiations; the secret of negotiation is to change that perception and in the process to change the stakes into items that can be used to benefit both parties. If the two nations involved in a dispute over a piece of land can come to see that what each is most interested in is the resources the land holds, then the two may be able to negotiate a deal whereby one can be the owner of the territory but the other will share in the benefits of the resources. Thus, each party can gain from the negotiation. In a positive sum situation each party comes out with some benefits; no one comes off unilaterally or exclusively best, but all parties come off better than before (even though one party may come off "more better" than the other).

These two perceptions were referred to by the British diplomatist, Sir Harold Nicolson (1964) as the personality types of Shopkeeper and Warrior. Nicolson saw Shopkeepers as men of goodwill and limited aims seeking positive-sum solutions, and Warriors as men of ill will and extended goals seeking their demands at the expense of the other party. But Nicolson also seems to suggest that agreement is always a good thing in itself, always possible, and that for the Shopkeeper there is always a mutually acceptable price for the goods. The fact is that sometimes the value of the goods is rightly high and more than willingness to agree is needed for an accord. Some interests are more vital and less negotiable than others, and rights may not be negotiable at all—just their applications may be. There must be a little Warrior in every successful Shopkeeper, and some way must be found to relate the two perceptions of values.

The second closely related concept, known as Homans's theorem, is the key to the accomplishment of a change from a zero-sum to a non-zero-sum situation. It says: "The more the items at stake can be divided into goods valued more by one party than they cost to the other and goods valued more by the other party than they cost to the first, the greater the chances of successful outcomes" (Homans 1961, p. 62). The notion of variable values implies that items are evaluated differently by different parties and also that these evaluations can be changed, by such devices as persuasion, inducement, alternatives, and reorganization of ideas. Negotiation is a matter of discovering and conveying these different evaluations, in the first phase, and of then mutually grouping and altering them so that they fit together into an agreement, in the second. This concept, and Homans's formulation of it, indicates that parties generally do not—and cannot—seek to prevail over the other's arguments by persuading them to change their basic views, but rather use persuasion to arrange the components of these views into a common decision.

The third concept is that of toughness and softness, or holding out and giving in, an old notion in the literature on negotiation. In the beginning of the eighteenth century, De Callières (1716, p. 42) expressed his admiration for the Cardinal d'Ossat because he "is firm as a rock when necessity demands [and] supple as a willow at another moment," but neither gentleman has ever revealed when those moments were. Two and a half centuries later, Bartos (1974) tried to draw some conclusions about the time for toughness and the time for softness, ending up primarily with a deeper understanding of the problems of the attempt. There are two aspects to the toughness–softness question; they must be separated for discussion, but each must be kept in mind while the other is being analyzed. One aspect is substantive: any decision on when to hold out and when to give in depends on the importance of the item at stake and the ability of a party to shave off a little bit in order to move in the direction of another party's wishes. This is the aspect already raised in regard to the Warrior in every Shopkeeper. The other aspect is procedural, referring to the process of negotiations: both toughness and softness have their moments, their meanings, their measures, and their manipulative effects. These are what make up the process of negotiation, the operations and possibilities that must be understood to bring different substantive viewpoints into one agreement. How and when to be tough or soft is one of the major questions of applied theory to be answered by the practical negotiator.

Nevertheless, this is not a handbook in the sense that it contains rules and recipes to follow, book in hand. Theory remains important, but the essence of negotiation is creativity, not legalisms. The analysis of the process and the behavioral prescriptions presented here have been stated as sharply as possible; otherwise they cannot be applied, tested, proven, or disproven. On occasion a particular situation may call for alternative analyses or strategies, some of them even mutually exclusive. The practitioner may be forced to combine or to choose, for not all the judgments will be equally or fully applicable. In all these cases, sharpness is preferred to a more cautious but probably less useful formulation. Yet the aim here is not to present a book of proverbs or commandments by which the game must be played. Rather it is to illuminate the constructive process and to stimulate creativity, to be a vehicle carrying negotiators beyond these prescriptions into the terrain of more inventive processes and more beneficial solutions.

2

The Practical Negotiator

Some people are good negotiators, and some are not; some are better at one particular type of negotiation than at others. Most people now consider President Woodrow Wilson, as imaginative and creative as he was, not to have been effective in negotiating a peace treaty. Several generations later, Secretary of State Henry Kissinger was lauded for his ability to conclude successfully several difficult negotiations. But what is it in the person who is doing the negotiating that makes the difference?

It is an axiom of this book that negotiators are made, not born, and that there is something about the process that can be taught and learned. But people learn things differently and they apply what they have learned in their own fashion according to their personalities. We have no intention of suggesting that personality tests should be administered to prospective negotiators or that only certain personality types should be chosen to be diplomats. We are not there yet, and many people may hope that we will never be there. An evaluation of an applicant's personality may be a factor in selection for diplomatic service, but it is not the only factor. There is not even a suggestion that negotiators can be typed to react in predictable ways. Psychology is a long way from being able to give such advice reliably. The best that can be said is that certain personality and attitude traits have been identified and are suspected of interacting in particular ways. Since personality typologies are still in a very tentative stage, the labels used here refer to rough categories of traits rather than distinct and established types. Some of the resulting interactions can be manipulated (assuming one knows one's own traits) and others have to be lived with.

Personality and attitudes have a role in shaping the way negotiators act and react. Personality refers to the more constant elements in an individual's psychological make-up; attitudes, perceptions, and behaviors are related to it but not inflexibly so. If the relationship were too close, if distinct personalities had fixed attitudes and behaviors, teaching skills and processes would be useless and personal interaction would literally be a matter of the "chemistry" of personality compounds. As it is, the interaction between personalities is mediated by a number of indeterminate elements, including both attitudes related to personality and processes independent of it. Negotiators work on this intermediate ground, where behaviors interact and influence each other.

LEARNING SKILLS

Contrary to the old saw that "an ambassador is an honest man sent abroad to lie for his country," Western diplomats insist strongly on the need for positive and even cooperative qualities in a negotiator. In interviews, a group of North American diplomats and students of negotiation associated with U.N. peacekeeping identified empathy and integrity as the negotiator's most important personal skills. Integrity, or trustworthiness, is discussed in a special section below. *Empathy* involves the crucial ability to understand the other party's point of view, if only in order to counter it more effectively, and encompasses both the intellectual and the emotional components of his stand. The diplomat who has developed enough credibility with negotiators of the other party to be able to tell them how their position is striking his side and advise them on the changes necessary to move both parties toward an agreement stands in the advantageous position of "mediator for his own side." Sympathy for the other's position would be too much to ask for and in any case would weaken a negotiator's ability to speak for his own side, but empathy means that he knows how his position looks from the other fellow's shoes, as well as how it feels to be in them.

W. Randolph Burgess, an American with a long diplomatic career, cautioned, "Try to understand the other side, so that you are not pushing people around. They should know you know their point of view as well" (Burgess interview). Charles Yost, who served as ambassador to the United Nations as well as to several countries, added:

> If you don't make an attempt to understand the other point of view, or your attempts fail, you're almost sure to miss out in negotiating unless you hold all the cards and can simply bully your way through. . . . The best negotiators have to have the right combination of pertinacity and tact—that is, they have to be able to push the central issues repeatedly and indefinitely if necessary, until a final solution is reached, but they have to do it with great understanding of the other side. (Yost interview)

Patience is also a factor that a number of experienced negotiators have stressed as a great asset. No matter how skilled a negotiator, many complex negotiations require long months and sometimes years to conclude. Adding to the need for patience is the fact that the duration of negotiations is so often unpredictable. Former President Gerald Ford commented on the need for great patience: "You can't go into negotiations and expect a very rapid resolution of differences. The differences are often very valid. They require gradual movement, and when you have gradual movement, it may take five hours, it may take five days or it may take longer" (Ford interview). The negotiations that ended the Korean war required two years and 575 meetings. The Austrian State Treaty negotiations took eight years and 400 meetings. The negotiations for the International Atomic Energy Agency lasted almost three years. The Law of the Sea was under debate for over a decade.

Since negotiation involves value change and accommodation, it is a learning process in which each party is both teacher and student, and that takes time. Beyond simply the time to talk out the complex problem and put together a solution to it, additional time is often needed to establish communications between parties. George Kennan is supposed to have proposed: "If you've decided your negotiations will take place in Geneva, then you take a year's lease on a nice house for your representative and you let him join the country club. *Then* he arranges to have a first meeting with the Russians." Within each party the same types of communications problems may also exist, again requiring patience from the waiting onlookers. Arthur Goldberg cited his experience in negotiating a space treaty with the Soviet Union:

> Everyone on our team agreed it was inconceivable that the poor Soviet Ambassador could ever have called up Marshal Gretchkov. He didn't have the access that we had to the power centers. He could not call Gromyko [either]. At the very best he would send a telegram to whomever was supervising the activity in the foreign office, who in turn would take it up through the hierarchical structure of the Soviet government. The United States is at a great

advantage in terms of speed, which is why I emphasize that you have to be patient in international negotiations. It takes an inordinate amount of time to resolve problems that look as if they should be resolved in a very short time. (Goldberg interview)

Self-assurance is another characteristic that many negotiators point to as being crucial in negotiations. Again in Goldberg's words, "Self-confidence obviously is required. If you don't have confidence in your own capacity, you're not a good negotiator. You're too timid. A certain courage is needed if you are to succeed at all as a negotiator" (Goldberg interview).

Yet self-confidence may be dependent on the knowledge that one is given full support at home for the conduct of negotiations. Goldberg continued, "Any negotiator must be supported in his negotiations. This is particularly true in the international area. Otherwise you will not get anywhere in a particular negotiation; and also your credibility—to use a very much abused word—as a negotiator will be impaired in other negotiations, because word will get around that you can't deliver on what you have negotiated" (Goldberg interview).

Ingenuity is an important factor cited by many negotiators. Put in practical terms, ingenuity is the ability to come up with arguments or proposals to overcome differences as they arise. More than repetition or rebuttal, new arguments have been shown to be the key to persuasion, and new proposals will be seen as crucial in forging parts of an agreement.

A complex negotiation over many issues places the negotiator in the position of being responsible for carrying out instructions and for protecting the interests of the nation and puts him under high stress. Negotiating sessions may go on for long hours, and it is not unknown for delegations to prolong sessions for the very purpose of wearing the other side down. Beyond patience, negotiators need endurance and strength under fire. Ambassador Goldberg felt strongly that

> a negotiator must have stamina—physical and mental stamina. He has got to be physically prepared, since he cannot always control the time of negotiations because other people are involved. He must not tire easily. I have seen very good people who are not good negotiators because their fatigue point is very low. I remember one example from the domestic scene. I could not use one of my best men after 10 o'clock at night. His fatigue point was low, and at that point he became irritable and almost developed mental blocks. He did not absorb what was going on, and there was just no use in having him around. And he was not an older member of the team. (Goldberg interview)

Stamina is needed for tenacity, which is sometimes more important than fine arguments. Harriman recalled a negotiating experience with Prince Sihanouk of Cambodia that required perseverance in tracking the prince down to agree to an American proposal:

> While attending a negotiating conference Sihanouk got up one day and said he was leaving the negotiations. . . . So I took a plane to Rome—I heard he was motoring down there—and I saw him the next evening. . . . I'll tell you how I did it. You have to be rather determined in such situations. His representatives in Rome couldn't tell me when he was going to arrive and they didn't know whether he could see me. I asked what hotel he was going to stay at, and they told me that. So I had a secretary from the American embassy sit in the lobby of the hotel, and I told him to stay there until Sihanouk arrived. When he

arrived, the secretary was to go up to him and say that I wanted to see him.

He arrived I think about 7 o'clock in the evening, and Sihanouk said that he wouldn't have any time to see me. I had told our man that he had to insist on it. So Sihanouk finally said that he would see me for 15 minutes. Well, I went there. We spent two hours. The net effect was that he sent his ambassador back to Geneva and signed the agreement at the end. He was tremendously flattered that I personally would do this. (Harriman interview)

Just as certain personal characteristics may account for an individual's effectiveness, others may limit his abilities to negotiate successfully. The need to be liked and be perceived as friendly may create what J. Robert Schaetzel, an American with extensive negotiating experience on economic matters, deemed a "mushy approach." He frequently deemed American negotiators to be "more interested in creating a friendly impression than in being accurate." Instead, "it is essential to create maximum clarity in terms of what the issues are and what the options are" (Schaetzel interview).

Robert Lovett, an American with a distinguished career in government, commented,

I think you have to be able to state things with reasonable simplicity and not get tangled up in long sentences and week-long paragraphs. It has to be very, very well drafted and redrafted, and again, I think you have to avoid making a subject too long. Once you've made your case, for God's sake, stop talking and sit down. That's where a lot of cases are lost. A negotiator is lost by making a point and then going on and sort of babbling on forever. You lose attention and you may lose points. (Lovett interview)

In the same vein, a negotiator must learn to avoid personalizing situations. As Lovett commented, "In certain types of negotiations you can't escape being pushed around, but you just don't take it personally, you don't let it bother you. Stick to the main objective and let the trivia go by you" (Lovett interview). So too must an effective negotiator be in control of his emotions. In Philip Jessup's words: "Occasionally it is valuable to appear to be very angry, but by and large, a cold kind of approach to a problem is I think more effective. One maxim is never to lose your temper unless you intend to" (Jessup interview). In the fourteen-week negotiations in London in the fall of 1979, in which the warring parties in Zimbabwe–Rhodesia struggled to reach an agreement, much of the credit for the successful outcome was given to Lord Carrington, the British Foreign Secretary. "Progress was made at the Lancaster House Talks," the *Economist* (December 15, 1979) observed, "only by setting deadlines and by Lord Carrington's studied impatience."

MEETING PERSONALITIES

Apart from the views of experienced practitioners who have had the opportunity to watch others negotiate and to conduct negotiations themselves, many experimental studies have investigated the relationship between particular personality traits or attitudes and bargaining behavior. Druckman (1973) has summarized these findings in a number of propositions:

1. The more complex, the more tense, and the clearer the definition of roles in a negotiating situation, the less likely will "person" variables (excluding "culture") affect negotiating behavior.
2. The more a negotiation situation permits a variety of "definitions" of purpose, opponent's intentions, and so on, the more likely will certain "person" variables affect negotiation behavior.
3. In situations which permit a variety of "definitions" those

"qualities" which affect perception of the specific situation, or are related to well-defined aspects of the situation, are most likely to affect negotiation behavior.

4. Altering situations (rather than selecting particular negotiators or altering the definition of diplomatic roles) is the most effective strategy for facilitating the achievement of satisfactory negotiated agreements.

5. In general, negotiation behavior is linked most closely to aspects of the immediate situation confronting negotiators (for example, other's strategy, outcome structure, threats).

The results are clear: On one hand, personality washes out in some situations as a predictor of behavior but, on the other, when it does operate it does so through the elements of strategy and tactics. It therefore becomes important to examine the traits and types that have been found to have some effect.

One attitudinal approach has sought to aggregate the many different types of traits that have been identified into a personality spectrum termed Interpersonal Orientation (IO), as summarized best by Rubin and Brown (1975, pp. 233–62). The two poles of the spectrum may be called "responsive" and "nonresponsive," reflecting their predispositions toward interaction with others and the role of that interaction in their view of the causes of human outcomes. The low or nonresponsive type pursues his goals independently of others in the way, is uninterested in the opponent as such, and sees the causes of human events in situations, forces, and mechanisms. Such a type may gain a lot for his side in negotiation, but he is not a "good" negotiator in the sense of creating an optimal result either through cooperation or through competition. The high or responsive type comes in two subtypes, the cooperative person who seeks a positive outcome by working with the other party to create it and expects others to reciprocate, and the competitive person who seeks a positive outcome by competing with the other party to create it and expects the other to do the same.

Given this threefold classification, various experiments have showed that the High Cooperative type usually favors abstract thinking, tolerates ambiguity, dislikes authoritarianism, accepts ethical flexibility, has a positive view of himself, and exhibits trustfulness and trustworthiness. On the other hand, the High Competitive type tends to have Machiavellian attitudes, to be suspicious, and to hold negative views of himself. The Low Interpersonal Orientation type will prefer concrete thinking, dislike ambiguity, exhibit authoritarianism, and avoid Machiavellianism and internationalism. If the negotiating party is a cooperative type, he will respond favorably to cooperation from the other side but he will tend to retaliate and react negatively to a competitive type. If the party negotiating has a competitive personality, he will relish a good challenge from another competitive type and both will do well, but he will consider a cooperative type a patsy and will try to exploit him. With a correct prior identification of personality types and correct behavior based on these types, the best results can be obtained. Such studies confirm in more scientific terms the intuitive insights of Sir Harold Nicolson, who wrote (1964, p. 26), "The greatest danger of all is the inability of the military school to understand the sincerity of the civilian school and the failure of the shopkeepers to realize that the warriors are inspired by a totally different idea of the means and purposes of negotiations. . . . This difference in conception creates, on one side, resentment; on the other, contemptuous suspicion."

Again, it should be emphasized that there is no notion of causation implied here nor any proof of exclusive correlations in all cases, but simply a repeated observation that these clusters of attitudinal or personality traits tend to go together. Much of this is confirmed common sense, but so is much of any scientific knowledge. There are lots of other correlations that might seem to make sense and that are not confirmed or are invalidated by careful observation (that is, experiments). However, precisely because of the need for controlled observation before making valid statements, it is much more difficult to find examples of these attitude clusters in the history of real cases. Colonel Mu'ammar Qaddafi, for example, appears to check out as a low IO, and in fact in the oil negotiations—notably those in 1970–71 soon after he came to power—he seemed to be interested in winning rather than compromising, uninterested in the opponents as such, and given to seeing forces, situations, and mechanisms as the adversary. Yet does this apply to 'Abdessalam Jallud, his second in command, whom many observers see as a very different personality from Qaddafi? And what about the other members of the Libyan delegation or government: are all Libyans low IOs? If so, should opponents refuse to negotiate, since low IOs are poor negotiators? The tool needs to be refined to be useful in drawing valid conclusions, and it would be hazardous for negotiators simply to type their adversaries and proceed accordingly. But the attitude clusters may be helpful in judging reactions, reducing surprises, and accounting for the way people react.

Another approach focuses on personality components seen in terms of basic needs, best developed in the work of Spector (1975, 1977) where personality needs are found to be good predictors of strategies and personality interaction is found to determine outcomes. Negotiators who use tactics involving promises to share items appear to be motivated by self-oriented personality needs for support, approval, and respect, particularly in situations where conflict is low. Other negotiators who rely on tactics involving promises to exchange items appear to be motivated by needs for play, cleverness, and exhibitionism; they are tempted to bluff and are low in their need for achievement. On a second level, dissimilar personalities (in terms of need orientations) tend to regard each other defensively and therefore to act cautiously and even cooperatively in interactions so as to avoid arousing hostility in the other party. Similar personality types, on the other hand, are likely to be less defensive, hence more competitive, aggressive, and even coercive toward each other. In other words, knowing that likes are expected to repel and unlikes to attract each other, the personality types react in such a way as to avoid triggering these mechanisms and being taken advantage of by them. This is quite the reverse of our intuitive behavior.

In sum, as the eighteenth-century writers and practitioners of negotiation like De Callières (1716) and De Felice (in Zartman, 1976) already noted, certain personality and attitude traits make for good negotiators. They should be oriented toward achievement but not aggressively hostile and should be friendly and conciliatory in appearance; they should not be impulsive, timid, or low in self-esteem. Unlike these earlier writers of popular psychology who focused on such traits in the abstract, psychologists today are studying traits in interaction. Spector's conclusions put the usefulness of these findings in the proper light: "If we come to the bargaining table knowing something about our counterpart—what motivates him, what his basic needs are, how he views the negotiation situation, what he expects us to do—we will be in an improved position to predict his choice of strategy and prepared to deal with him and reach an early and favorable agreement" (1977, p. 27).

BUILDING TRUST

Some of the concern about personality and attitude traits comes down to the matter of trust, one of the cardinal underlying characteristics of a fruitful negotiation. Many negotiators make comments such as those of Ambassador Kenneth Rush: "I've often seen negotiations deadlock because of emotional conflicts and distrust" (Rush interview); and experiments like those of Morton Deutsch (1974) focus on trust as the key element in reaching a satisfactory agreement. As with other elements of negotiation, starting with the basic contradiction between conflict and cooperation, trust involves a paradox. Friendly, cooperative, problem-solving sessions are built on trust as a jointly shared virtue. But even in hostile conflictual situations where each party is out to get the most, if not all, in the final settlement, each also seeks to dissimulate hostility and conflict and induce trust in the other party, if only to permit bluffing, lulling, and, finally, lopsided agreement. Moreover, it is in the interest of the sharpest, most antagonistic negotiator to sincerely foster feelings of trust, since discovery of false deadlines and bad faith destroys the element he needs to draw a sharp bargain. In other words, *the more a negotiator wants to bluff, the more he needs to appear trustworthy in order to carry off his deception when its moment comes.*

On the other hand, it is always tempting to any negotiator to abuse (perhaps it would be better to say "stretch") trust a little since there are occasions when a valuable edge can be won by bluffing. Thus, no party can be completely trusting, since he would be at the mercy of the other's deceptions, and no party can be completely untrustworthy, since he would destroy the possibility of any agreement. Because agreements involve future contingencies and outcomes, which are separate from and subsequent to the actual agreement, trust is necessary. Despite representations of negotiators as wily and Machiavellian, many point to the absolute essentiality of integrity. Schaetzel commented on his extensive experience in negotiating with Europeans, "Integrity is so obvious that no one is prepared to question it. Even in the sharpest negotiations you will have the Europeans saying, 'I am having great difficulty but I have complete trust in this man. I know that he is absolutely honest in what he is trying to do'" (Schaetzel interview).

Trust is merely a matter of credibility, whether it concerns information on past events or intentions about future contingencies. There are a number of ways in which credibility can be improved, although of course none by which it can be assured. The major means of improving trust about past information is simply to establish a record of verifiability, including the use of independent sources of information or even of the other party's sources. If the negotiator is caught in a bluff it will damage his credibility and impair his credentials in future negotiations with the same party. As Schaetzel commented, the requirement of a successful negotiator is "complete honesty in trying to develop an appreciation on each side of the limits that surround its ability to compromise" (Schaetzel interview). Or as Harriman put it: "If you want to come to an agreement, you want to pick a fellow who has a reputation on the other side—it may not have to be very publicly known—of being fair and wanting to reach agreements. Whereas if you appoint a man who does not have this fair reputation, you may sacrifice progress in the negotiation" (Harriman interview).

Negotiators themselves often point to the positive impact that a good personal working relationship can have on a negotiation and a negotiator's credibility. Contacts away from the bargaining table in a relaxed atmosphere may contribute to the creation of good working relations. One potential benefit from direct face to face meetings of heads of state at summit parleys is the creation of personal working relationships, as mentioned by former President Gerald Ford in an interview conducted after he left the presidency:

> I think summit meetings between heads of government to establish a personal relationship are important. In the

case of a number of people that I met who were heads of government—whether Mr. Brezhnev, President Giscard, Chancellor Schmidt, Prime Minister Wilson, Prime Minister Callaghan, Sadat, Rabin and others—I worked better, and I think it's to the mutual advantage of both, to have that face-to-face exposure and experience. . . . I developed following these personal meetings a capability to call, and I did, virtually every head of government if we had a problem, and the initial personal exposure to one another made it easier to talk via long distance or to write and communicate by letter. . . . And there's something about that relationship which makes it easier to understand their point of view and they to understand our point of view. (Ford interview)

But there are limits to the role that personal credibility plays. Although President Ford commented on the benefits of face-to-face summits, he also expressed his opinion that they ought not be held repetitively just for the relationship. In Philip Jessup's words: "If you had very friendly relations with your opposite number, if he had instructions he might be able to tell you that those were his instructions and personally he disagreed, but this is different from assuming that just by being nice you are going to get the fellow over on your side." Jessup also recounted an incident that demonstrated the limitations of the personal relationship:

In 1947 I was on the committee to draw up a plan for the International Law Commission, and the Russian representative on the committee was Koretzsky, who was later my congenial colleague on the International Court. And while we were on the committee we worked very closely together—he was very accommodating and he would come to lunch or dinner with us, and he mixed very freely. The next year he came back with the Delegation, in 1948, to the Assembly, and when I first greeted him I greeted him very warmly and I said, "How about having lunch today?" And he said, "Oh no, I am very busy, thank you." "Well, how about tomorrow?" "No." And so with every approach we made. I remember Chip Bohlen warning us that this was a constant phenomenon, that the instructions from the Kremlin would be, "This year you be friendly and hobnob with people, and see what you get out of that." Otherwise it was "this year we are going to be cold and stand them off." (Jessup interview)

Trust and credibility are important if each side is to feel sure of the other side's desire to reach a negotiated outcome. In 1969 Arthur Goldberg commented that the problem with the administration's position in the Vietnam negotiations in Paris was its lack of credibility:

The other side has to believe that your position is a credible position. . . . The Vietnamization program of the administration runs exactly contrary to the position that we do not want a military victory. We entered in full force in Vietnam with our 500,000 troops on the assumption that the South Vietnamese could not carry on that war and would collapse if we did not send substantial forces into Vietnam. . . . Considering that the object was . . . to hold the fort until the South Vietnamese could do it themselves, it would be a complete military victory if we were able to succeed in this program. Now, that's not credible to the other side in a negotiating sense. We say we don't want a military victory. . . . But they add it up. They'd be foolish not to add it up. I'd add it up in the same way. I would say that this program which was announced is a program for a military victory. (Goldberg interview)

In the same vein, a party's stated willingness for a

negotiated outcome may lack credibility because of the quality of representation at a negotiation. Goldberg also noted:

> You cannot have a successful negotiation on Vietnam by giving Averell Harriman's third assistant, a very nice foreign service officer and a very capable and able man, the title of the personal rank of ambassador and lead the other side to the belief that you are genuinely interested in negotiations. I've found in negotiating with Communists that protocol is as important to them as it is to union people. If the head of an outfit is a prestigious man, they will send a key negotiator. If you downgrade the negotiations, they will send an inferior negotiator. And in each instance there will be a deterioration in the negotiation process. (Goldberg interview)

The same mistake was made by North Vietnam in March 1972 in the Kissinger negotiations, leading the United States to break off talks and both sides to return to the battlefield.

Trust and negotiated agreement are intertwined, to the point where neither is possible without the other. Yet trust cannot be a precondition to negotiation, no matter how useful it may be. One cannot stop negotiating and create trust before continuing; it must be built up as part of the process of coming to an agreement.

Trust about future intentions is complicated, primarily because there is no verifiability until it is too late. A good record helps, as Harriman mentioned, but there must be other ways of assuring predictability, some of which will be spelled out here. Like any book of proverbs, some of these guidlines may be overlapping or contradictory, leaving the parties either with the need to identify appropriate moments or with an open choice.

Trust is enhanced if a negotiator demonstrates a capacity

to understand the problems of the other side and help solve them, and brings his own problems as well.

Sympathy is outside the job description of a negotiator but empathy is important. The ability to listen to the demands and positions of the other, to enter into his confidence and to take him into one's own, may all appear as cosmetic but may have real impact on the substance of the agreement.

Trust is enhanced if a negotiator can demonstrate a genuine interest in trying to help the other side reach its objective while retaining his own objective and making the two appear compatible.

If one appears to be giving away too many points deemed crucial to one's case, distrust may result instead, but if the goals of the two parties can be shown to be similar or complementary, or even if information is exchanged to that end, trust can be enhanced (Pruitt et al. 1978, Kimmel et al. 1980, Carnevale et al. 1979).

Trust is enhanced by not threatening or promising wildly.

Side payments must be offered seriously, leaving the impression that they will be carried out; initial positions must be reasonable, not irresponsible, conveying a sense of limited and credible aims. Wild pressures and exaggerated openers destroy trust by raising doubts about the permanence of any agreement that is necessarily much less than the initial demands. This factor differentiates Israeli–Egyptian from Israeli–Syrian relations during the disengagement talks and after.

Trust is enhanced by step-by-step agreements with "accounting points" along the way.

If parties know that they can stop and check several times before arriving at the final irrevocable outcome, their trust increases and they know that the other party, thinking the same way, will be less likely to default (Pruitt 1981, ch. 6). However, the first items must include some of the major problems to be solved, or the perception will be that the tougher issues are being postponed and the result will be no trust at all. The essential core of Kissinger's step-by-step negotiations in the Mideast was the creation of trust through partial agreements in which the parties simply had to have confidence in each other. A less well-known example of steps to create trust was a missed opportunity in the Vietnam negotiations as recalled by Averell Harriman:

> You don't always have to have agreements. You can come to understandings through mutual example. In other words, at one point in the war the North Vietnamese took eleven regiments of the twenty-five they had in the northern two provinces 200 miles north of the DMZ. They took another eight just north of the DMZ, and three in Laos. They only left three in the country. They disengaged to such an extent that Abrams took the First Cavalry Division down to the Third Corps to increase our activity there. Now, I think if the Saigon government had joined the Paris negotiations at that time and we had had the two sides with the four participants, we would have been able to work rather rapidly towards a mutual reduction of violence. I base that on what they did at the time; the fact that they took eleven regiments north would have justified our taking some troops home. (Harriman interview)

Trust is enhanced by "free offers" to trust.

If one party willingly offers the other minor occasions where it is at the mercy of the other, indicating its view of the other as trustworthy, it implants the notion of trust in the proceedings. (Pruitt 1981, ch. 6). After all, the bow, the handshake, the salute, and the tip of the hat are all medieval indications of trust in the other party through a gesture of voluntary defenselessness. Nothing better illustrates this point than the visit of President Sadat to Jerusalem in November 1977, where the diplomatically risky initiative was a free offer of trust that pressed trust on the other party. A less dramatic example was the Pakistani announcement, on June 27, 1972—the day before the Simla conference between the two parties opened—that it was ready to resume diplomatic relations with India, making a free concession without waiting for repayment in order to create trust.

Trust is enhanced when a party would be taking the proffered action anyhow.

If a party can show that it would be doing the promised activity in any case, it may reduce that action's value as a concession but it will increase the other's willingness to believe the action will take place. The problem then becomes one of reinforcing the predictability of the future intention.

Trust is enhanced when a party can show or be shown that the action is in its interest.

Again, it is a question of establishing future intentions by giving reasons for their implementation. If a party can be motivated or show that it is already motivated to carry out the action by itself, even if it had no previous intention of doing so, the chances of its doing so and thus the chances of the other party believing it are increased (Loomis 1959). The agreement may provide good reasons for this motivation. The problem has long plagued Russian-American relations: "We should try to obtain promises which the Soviet Union itself will have a definite incentive to keep, either because the promise is consistent with Soviet national interests or because of the impact of world opinion. In any case, we must always be on guard against trading concrete political, economic, and military assets of our own for the unsupported promises of the Soviet Union" (Kohler 1958, p. 906). Israel has felt the same way about trusting Arab countries.

Trust is enhanced when there are no (other) preferred alternatives.

If there is no other way of arriving at the indicated outcomes, no other way for the party to act, or at least no less costly alternative, the chances are that the party will take the promised course. Although this is a logical banality, it points to the fact that parties can use this condition in their arguments in order to increase the credibility of their commitments.

Trust is enhanced when a party agrees to punish violators.

In perfect trust no punishment is necessary because no violations are envisaged. In the absence of perfect trust, to suggest or agree to verification and sanction procedures to which the party itself would be liable if it broke trust is a way of suggesting that such a breach is not envisaged. Certainly a major problem with the Soviet refusal of inspection and verification in disarmament agreements is that it strongly suggests that the Russians intend to break the treaty; trust might be restored if it were conclusively shown that the refusal is for other reasons. More broadly, trust is enhanced when parties have a clear idea of what the other will do if trust is fulfilled or is broken. Benefits and sanctions must in their turn be credible, but if appropriate they add concreteness to the future contingency. If any of the signatories to the 1963 Test-Ban Treaty or other arms limitations agreements break the agreement, consequences such as the probability of similar actions from other parties are well known. By the same token, the fact that there have been numerous alleged violations of the SALT agreements by the Russians and that Secretary Kissinger supposedly turned a blind eye to them in the name of detente created distrust both in the agreements and in the accountability system.

Trust is enhanced when interdependence is increased.

If the benefits a party promises are inextricably linked to the benefits the party itself receives, the chances of default are reduced. This is easier to accomplish when one is allocating a newly created good (even an abstract one, like peace) than when one is about to share a good that was formerly an exclusive possession. But however arrived at, the provision of mutual gratification or mutual deprivation improves credibility about the shared item (Pruitt 1981, ch. 5). One of President Sadat's points of emphasis in his negotiations with the Israelis in late 1977 and early 1978, at least as judged from his public statements, was that both nations stood to gain from peace and that both could lose without it.

Trust is enhanced when there is an early return on the agreement.

Even if the full benefits of the agreements do not appear until much later, some immediate benefits paid from one party to the other will help the latter believe in the full agreement and will help engage its responsibility as well. Soon after the meetings between President Sadat and Prime Minister Begin in late 1977, Israeli journalists were allowed to visit Egypt for the first time. This precedent was given much attention in the press of both nations as an early payoff of the negotiations.

Within the process of institutionalizing trust between the parties, a more personal trust can also grow up among members of opposing delegations. As discussions continue they may develop a personal identification with the success of the negotiations and start to help each other to sell an agreement to their home governments. Indeed, for this reason many foreign ministries enforce rotation of members of delegations.

Theodore Achilles, a member of the U.S. delegation that drafted the Atlantic Treaty, recalled the close working relationship that prevailed among the various delegations during those negotiations.

At first there were the British, French, Belgians, Dutch, Luxembourgers, Canadians, and ourselves. The negotiations were normally conducted by the Secretary of State and the various ambassadors in Washington. They met only infrequently. The actual negotiations were conducted by a working group of which Jack Hickerson was the senior U.S. member, Bill Galloway the junior officer, and [which included] myself and two other members of the U.S. team. The other members were ministers or political counselors of the various embassies here.

That was before the days of air conditioning, and we met all summer in our shirt sleeves around a table in one of the offices of the State Department. By the time the summer was over we had a treaty in pretty good shape, and all knew each other intimately, trusted each other, and we were all used to working together. Derick Hoyer-Miller, who was the British minister and the senior member of the British representatives in the working group, started something which we later called the NATO spirit. One day in a working group he made a proposal. No one remembers what it was, but nobody liked the proposal and we all said so rather bluntly. And Derick said, "All right, those are my instructions from London. I'll tell them that I made my pitch and that it was shot down, and that this is what everybody else thinks the answer should be."

So we worked out collectively what we thought the best arrangement was. Derick referred it back to London and got approval on it, and we all referred it to our various governments and got approval.

That developed into quite a negotiating technique. No matter what any of us had by way of instruction, we would try to find what we thought was the right answer, and then tried to get our respective governments to agree to it. That worked out very well indeed.

When the permanent NATO organization was being set up in London—I was our representative on one committee—some of the people there had been members of our working group and some had not, and our French opposite number on the committee had not; he was just coming fresh into the picture. He made a proposal at one point. I'd forgotten that he was a newcomer and I said, "That makes no sense. How about this?" He looked at me rather annoyed and he said, "Well, those are my instructions." I said, "Yes, I know, but they are wrong. Get them changed." He looked at me, amazed this time, thinking, perhaps, this American must be crazy, he doesn't realize that I have to carry out my instructions. Well, we passed over that point. A little bit later I had to make a proposal under instructions that I didn't like. The Frenchmen and others said they didn't like it, and I said, "Those are my instructions, but I don't think it's a good idea and I'll see if I can get them changed." At this point the Frenchman almost exploded—Is this American crazy, or is he a master of duplicity, or what in the world is he trying to do? It just never occurred to him that negotiations should be carried out that way. But it worked. (Achilles interview)

There are many instances when the element of trust between negotiators—even those coming from countries that are not allies—has made a difference. Lord Caradon, formerly British Permanent Representative to the United Nations, recalls such an incident:

> In 1967 when we put forward a British resolution, 242, on the Middle East, we worked of course not only in the corridors and offices of New York, but in all the capitals of the world, the telegrams were going, and we worked over a period of weeks. I thought we had the nine votes in the [Security] Council and we had worked for it and we thought we had got it. We were going in to take the vote on the Monday, when on the Sunday night they called up from my delegation and said, "It's no use." I said, "What's happened?" They said, "At this last moment there is a Russian resolution put down, clearly a wrecking resolution, an extreme resolution."
>
> You go down the next day, in the evening, for the vote. People wait for you to try and get you to make the last minute amendments. No, you can't wait any longer. I still think I have the nine votes.
>
> Then Deputy Foreign Minister Kuznetzov wants to see me. I greatly respect him. Could he see me alone? Certainly. So we go into a little room by the Security Council, and he says at once, "I want you to give me two days." And I say, "Look, ask me anything else, but don't ask me that. We haven't been to bed for several nights and I don't suppose you have either. We've got the nine votes, I think."
>
> I wasn't quite sure, actually, since we hadn't heard from the Latin Americans—we needed the two Latin American votes for the nine. You speak very frankly together on such occasions. And then he said, "I am not sure you understand what I am saying to you. I am personally asking you for two days."
>
> So I wonder what my delegation will think or what

my Government will think about it, but I go back into the Council and say that at this last moment a request has been made for a postponement of this all-important vote, and I ask for an adjournment till Wednesday evening.

On the Wednesday you go down—there can't be any postponements now. The first question you ask is, "Who is down to speak?" Syria is down to speak. Then as the long Syrian speech comes toward an end you realize that no one is going to speak. They are all a bit confused by the Russian resolution that had been put down the previous Sunday night.

You proceed to the vote, and you vote by raising your hand as you know. You raise your right hand in support of the British resolution because it was down first. Then there is a sort of ragged cheer from the back of the press gallery, and then you realize that it's a unanimous vote. The Russians too voted for the British resolution; that's why he was asking me for the two days. He couldn't have asked me in those terms unless he was going to work with the rest of the delegates; actually I didn't expect him to do more than to abstain. But when he said, "I am personally asking you for two days," he meant that he was not out to wreck my own initiative; he wanted time to refer back to his government to get support for our resolution. What he was saying to me was a question of trust; it all depended on working together. (Caradon interview).

3

Bringing about Negotiations: The Diagnostic Phase

Long before the first formal session opens, the negotiation process begins with the decision made by each party to explore the possibility of negotiating. This moment is usually not nearly as clear-cut as the word "decision" would suggest. First contacts and soundings frequently lie buried in the day-to-day exercise of diplomacy or in the conflict itself. Since ongoing communications are a permanent characteristic of relations in a world that includes not only thousands of diplomats but the media, international organizations, and nongovernmental groups and exchanges, it is usually difficult and often fruitless to try to locate the exact moment when such contacts began. In special cases, it is true, a party may agree to begin formal negotiations with no expectation or even desire to see a negotiated settlement. The Japanese entered into negotiations with the United States at the same time that their attack on Pearl Harbor was in the making. The negotiations provided a good cover. It is still not clear whether South Africa was interested in finding a negotiated solution to replace its plans for Namibian independence between 1977 and 1981 or whether it learned in the process that a negotiated solution was unacceptable. In many other cases, discussions begun in doubt can open the way to successful negotiation. SALT I and the Golan Heights disengagement agreement, among many others, began that way.

Nevertheless, the beginning of the negotiating process does generally imply that there have been conscious and essentially volitional changes in the way things are perceived, whether a special moment can be identified with these changes or not. Sometimes a change in approach may be signaled by a dramatic event, such as Egyptian President Sadat's announcement of his plan to visit Jerusalem. At other times the change may be gradual and quieter.

Not all issues are negotiable at a given time. The parties in conflict may refuse to communicate, and in that event no negotiation is possible. Even if they are willing to communicate, directly or through other parties, the issue itself may still be non-negotiable. The reasons can be considered either objective or subjective, depending on one's view of perception and reality and one's standpoint on the issue itself. Parties who are ready to negotiate an issue see non-negotiability as a purely subjective problem of the other side. "It is the intransigence of the other side that prevents us from finding the obvious solution," they might say. "President Mohammed Siad Barre of Somalia said that he saw no chance of a negotiated settlement with Ethiopia to end the war over the Ogaden region in the horn of Africa," the *New York Times* (January 30, 1978) reported. "He said control of the fighting had passed from Ethiopian hands to the Soviet Union. . . . No one will be able to convince the Soviet Union to stop the war."

Parties who are not ready to negotiate may consider non-negotiability to be an objective obstacle inherent in the issue itself: "There is no way of reconciling positions in this conflict; we're on a collision course." They may also project the blame onto the subjective unwillingness of the other side, which forms a part of the "objective structure" of the conflict. "We have always been willing to negotiate," said the Israelis for many years, "but the Arabs are unable to do so because of their divisions and weakness, so it is useless for us to pursue the path of conciliation."

There is not much to be done if a party refuses to negotiate. The other party may try to change its opponent's perception of the issue, in ways to be discussed later in this chapter, but if the opponent refuses even to consider that a mutually agreeable solution may be possible, of course it is not possible. As long as the Americans and the North Vietnamese, the Greeks and the Turks, the French and the Algerians, the Egyptians and the Israelis, and many others—or any one party in these pairs—felt that there was no possible mutually agreeable solution to the Vietnamese, Cypriot, Algerian, Sinai, or any other problem, there was none. Objectively, there may have been many conceivable outcomes that lay somewhere "between" the demands of the two sides, but the denial of one or both sides prevented them from being realized. Yet in each case, and in many others, it became apparent at some point that such solutions might exist, and as a consequence of that recognition the veto was lifted and a single mutually agreed solution was found through negotiation. At that point both parties perceived that on one or more issues their common interests exceeded their conflicting interests or at least that their common interest in some agreement outweighed their conflicts on specific issues.

While the citation of even an infinite number of examples could not prove that a negotiated settlement is available for every problem, historical evidence does show that even many of those issues which, objectively, seemed the most impervious to negotiations were finally resolved. For some problems this is not the case. Throughout the Munich negotiations, Prime Minister Neville Chamberlin thought that negotiation was possible, and he returned to England saying, "I have brought peace in our time." He soon recognized what others had seen earlier—that a limit on Hitler's demands could not be attained through negotiation. In order to reach a mutually agreeable outcome, both parties must be prepared to move from original unacceptable positions. If parties are unwilling to do so, or if they perceive their opponents as unbudging on fundamental issues, there can be no real negotiation. But these are subjective considerations.

A dispute may remain non-negotiable if all parties do not perceive that they would be better off with an agreement than in the absence of one. To have a successful negotiation, in the words of Ambassador Kenneth Rush, who has negotiated extensively in business and diplomacy, "both parties must feel they want to make an agreement. If you push someone, for example, into buying something that he doesn't want, you may sell him that one thing, but from then on your relation with him will not continue" (Rush interview).

The negotiability of an issue is therefore ultimately a subjective matter of perception and will. As Vladimir Velebit, who represented Yugoslavia in the successful negotiation of a once intractable dispute over Trieste, phrased it, "I am certain there is no such problem, no such conflict in the world which cannot be settled if both sides are determined to find a settlement" (Campbell 1976, p. 105). At this point in the argument we are not saying that a particular solution exists and is recognized by the parties (a situation that would refer to the end, not the beginning, of the process), but simply that the possibility of a solution must be recognized for the negotiation process to begin.

RECOGNIZING OPPORTUNITIES

When is negotiation an appropriate way of handling a conflict? The characteristics that lead parties to define issues as negotiable can be described in a number of ways, referring to different but related aspects of the nature and process of negotiation. The very fact that there are so many ways of answering the question provides an opportunity for parties trying to overturn the obstacles that keep them from coming to an agreement. If they cannot find a convincing answer in one set of terms, they can try others as they seek to change the subjective evaluations of their opponent.

To Make New Decisions

In general, situations appropriate for negotiation have two characteristics: the parties agree that they need a solution ("We can't go on like this any longer") and that their decision on a solution must be unanimous ("We're all in this together, like it or not"). The two go together—"We had to get together on a new solution," and "A solution had to be found that we could all accept." These are the characteristics that make negotiation different from other decision-making processes.

Negotiation is appropriate when decisions must be unanimous.

Negotiation is different from two other types of decision-making characterized by equally simple rules. When the parties involved in making a decision agree to abide by a numerical *majority* on a specific alternative, they have established a rule called *voting*. Or when they agree, explicitly or tacitly, to abide by the *judgment* of another party, the rule may take on a variety of names according to the qualities of the judge (arbitration, *diktat*, adjudication, and so forth) but the predominant characteristic is the recognition of *authority*.

Negotiation is appropriate when there is neither authority nor majority but when unanimity is the decision rule.

Or, reversing the identification, one can say that when there are no fixed alternatives to vote up or down, when there is no agreement to equate numbers with power, and when there is no recognized authority to make a decision, the issue needs to be decided by negotiation since there is no agreement on the procedures by which to produce an agreement on the substance. Of course, these characteristics alone do not tell whether the parties involved perceive an issue to be negotiable, merely that negotiation is the appropriate process for arriving at a decision. On the other hand, they do help us to understand why negotiation is used among sovereign equal parties who do not recognize a higher authority and cannot be forced to comply with the terms of an agreement—a characterization that applies both to relations among states and also (perhaps surprisingly) to labor–management relations (except in those instances where the government has the power to step in and force the parties to come to agreement).

These characteristics also draw attention to a point that will prove crucial in the following discussions, namely, that negotiations involve above all the discovery (or invention) of new alternatives rather than the choice between fixed, given options. Thus:

> *Negotiation is appropriate when new solutions have to be invented to replace unacceptable old ones or new ones have to be created when new problems arise.*

This may mean that old solutions have to be presented in a new light, but more often it means that new ones have to be found.

To Create New Orders

A more historical way of saying the same thing is:

> *Negotiation is appropriate when there is a change in*

*the structure of affairs and a new order must be created
or problems managed in its absence.*

History has been marked by "ages of negotiation," periods when diplomacy is called into exceptional activity.
Often these take place after a war, when a new international
order has to be built out of the wreckage; the rounds of conferences in Vienna, Versailles, and San Francisco that followed the Napoleonic Wars and World Wars I and II are
examples. At other times, an age of negotiation marks a
broader change in the international order, even beyond the
effects of a single war. The various negotiations taking place
during the 1980s are part of the process of replacing a
number of previous international orders—the colonial system, the bipolar system, and the economic order established
by the industrialized nations during the nineteenth century.

Access of new groups to the negotiating table is often the
first major indication of a passing international order. Even
before discussing the substance of a new order, new potential members want to share in the procedures of creating it. A
Third World economist captured this duality well when he
spoke of negotiating a new relationship with the rich nations
through the instrument of collective bargaining: "The essence of this new deal lies in the objective of the developing
countries to obtain greater equality of opportunity and to
secure the right to sit as equals around the bargaining tables
of the world" (Ul-Haq 1976, p. 158). A seat at the table is an
indication that one side views the other as a party to be reck-
oned with, although it does not necessarily indicate willingness to enter into negotiations with it. The appearance of
listening to the developing nations' claims may be used as a
device to delay the search for mutually acceptable solutions
to economic problems, and talking together may be used to
educate the other party rather than to exchange concessions
(Erb 1975, p. 143). Nonetheless, while an expressed willing-

ness to enter into negotiations may be intended as a way of forestalling new orders rather than creating them, the expression of willingness does in fact create procedures which in the long run can lead to changes of substance.

Systems of world order provide the framework or structure for the conduct of international relations, including the use of negotiation as a mechanism for problem-solving. But when the world order systems themselves need replacing, or when power relations change within a system, the need for negotiation is even greater, since even the minimal rules of procedure that existed before are liable to be called into question. Not only do new parties seek membership in the system, but old definitions and criteria of power are questioned, new issues are introduced, established ways of making decisions are challenged. The rules and relations break down and need revision because of the changes in the relative power of the parties, discussed in the next section. Borders have often been the ultimate test of power relations. Countries battle and then negotiate to make their boundaries reflect their relative power. Even as recently as early 1979, Chinese and Vietnamese fought over both territory and its legal basis in a system of international relations. Vietnam insisted that Chinese troops withdraw "to the other side of the historical borderline which the two sides had agreed to respect," as a precondition for negotiations. China viewed this line as the result of an unequal treaty from an imperialist era, imposed by the French colonial ruler of Indochina on the Qing dynasty in 1887 and 1895 and wanted the line itself to be a subject of negotiation. China and India, Morocco and Algeria, and Ethiopia and Somalia have had the same problems.

Negotiations are needed whenever any structure of relations is changed, not only in the diplomatic area; business mergers, growing up in a family, and executive hiring are other cases. Of course, even when a particular structure of relations is not undergoing change and challenge, negotiation is likely to serve as a mechanism of solving problems and reducing conflict in the absence of formal decision rules or preparatory to their application. Such is frequently the case in labor–management bargaining, legislative drafting sessions on bills, personnel grievance disputes, plea bargaining, and so on.

To Seize on Change

Negotiation is appropriate when propitious changes have taken place.

Diplomatic writers from the seventeenth century were always telling their readers to learn to seize upon the right moment, but such advice is a little flat unless it tells how to identify the right moment.

Among the types of propitious changes are a change in attitudes and a change in the holders of attitudes. The latter is easier to identify. When a government which refused to negotiate is defeated or otherwise replaced, some discreet soundings are in order. Obvious as this may seem, it is not always observed. A party may be so locked into its view of the preceding government that it does not make the necessary demarche. The opposite danger is that a demarche may not be made discreetly enough and the opposite party is caught off balance, even if it was somewhat favorable to negotiations (although it is true that various degrees of "going public" may also be useful in nailing down a commitment that secrecy would keep vague). President Sadat selected late fall 1977, when a new Israeli government had recently come to office, to introduce his dramatic peace proposal. Usually, however, it is the new incumbent who makes the demarche.

The identification of changes in attitude in the same personnel is more difficult, to the point where one may say that it is as much of an art to recognize changes as it is to produce them. Introducing a new initiative at a point when it captures a change of heart in the other side's decision-makers is crucial, whether the source of change lies in outside events or in one's own tactics. An American active in arms negotiations over two decades has noted that the initiative of President Kennedy in his American University speech in June 1963, telling the Russians that "We won't test unless you do" came at just the right moment. "There can be long breaks before there is any movement on the other side, and it is a matter of deciding when they are ready to move before you give away something" (Fisher interview). Lord Caradon, British Permanent Representative in the United Nations during the Arab-Israeli conflict in 1967, told why the timing was right for the initiative that led to Resolution 242 in November 1967 when efforts during the previous summer had been unproductive:

> The Russians called a special meeting of the Assembly and for a month or more we sat in the Assembly that summer. Nothing came out of it at all except bad feeling and bad language, and we were much worse off at the end of the General Assembly than we were at the beginning. There was therefore the mere frustration of that delay that lent itself to a new effort. . . . I can't explain why at that particular time, but it was the time, I suppose, when the frustrations of the Assembly during the summer contributed, perhaps, to the good fortune of timing as far as we were concerned, because people realized that something really must be done about this. (Caradon interview)

Particularly in time of conflict, one party may have difficulty in perceiving the other party's inclination toward negotiation and may concentrate instead on pursuing the conflict. At the peak of the General Electric union—management conflict of 1962, acrimony led to a blurring of real issues and the focusing of attention on labels rather than on existing problems, thus adding stereotyping to all the other obstacles to problem-solving (Blake and Mouton in Sherif 1962, p. 102). In international disputes, parties often get so bogged down in charges and countercharges that the possibility of resolving the disputes or even attaining one's goal becomes lost in the drama. Pride and public image become so involved that the parties dare not admit any flexibility, so they never move to test whether the other's attitudes may have changed.

Averell Harriman criticized the Nixon administration in 1969 for its failure to recognize conciliatory gestures coming from the North Vietnamese:

> [The Administration] expects the North Vietnamese to come in and inform us that their lull in the fighting has a political significance. They'll never do that. Their position is that we are the aggressor, we've got to get our troops out, they're not going to pay any attention or negotiate on that subject until we do it. We have to accept that. We have to take certain risks, if you want to put it that way. They disengaged in the northern provinces of I Corps in South Vietnam at one point. It was perfectly obvious that this was a disengagement, and our military advisors in Paris agreed that it was, but MACV in Saigon and the Joint Chiefs of Staff said, "We have no proof— we've got 'em licked." (Harriman interview)

Changes in attitudes toward negotiation usually come about through a comparative evaluation of present and future possibilities.

The moment is propitious for negotiation when both sides perceive that they may be better off with an agreement than without one.

The outcome without an agreement—technically referred to as the party's security point—is an important point of reference in thinking about negotiations. It is important for the tactics of persuasion when one is trying to sell particular terms in negotiation, as will be discussed later, and it is also important for the initial decision to negotiate. There are variable security points, since there is more than one basis for an estimate of the value and meaning of non-agreement—What if talks broke off now? What if talks had never begun? What if some other way were tried to reach the goal? and so forth. However, parties usually pick one—or at most, a few—outcomes to which to compare the advantages of negotiation. People usually perceive selectively, and decision-makers usually reduce uncertain futures to a manageable number when deciding a course of action. Parties may of course see different outcomes in the same situation, or value the same outcome differently, or they may both see the same outcome and consider it worse for themselves than a possible negotiated agreement.

For example, one party may feel that the unacceptable alternative lies with the whole flow of time that is working against him—as Prime Minister Ian Smith did in Rhodesia when he decided to seek a negotiated solution while he still had power, lest he lose both present power and future possibilities—while the other side feels that the alternative of future effort and uncertainty may be less desirable than conceivable negotiated terms—as did some Zimbabwe nationalists at various times in the same situation. Nine such attempts failed before 1979 but the Lancaster House talks succeeded in bringing Zimbabwe recognized independence because both sides came to the talks considerably weakened. After seven years of war neither side felt it could win soon. Even the Muzorewa–Smith government could not achieve the international recognition it needed and the Patriotic Front forces had suffered heavy attacks on their sanctuaries. To both, the costs and prospects of continuing war were

more burdensome than the costs and prospects of a negotiated settlement.

Or both parties may come to feel that the alternative is the
same undesirable situation, such as the unwinnable war, as
the American government did sometime during 1969 and
the North Vietnamese Politburo did in the summer of 1972.
The change may also come about through interested third
parties, who perceive one future scenario to be the alternative solution that is unavoidable except by negotiation.
Western members of the U.N. Security Council undertook to
negotiate a governmental transition in Namibia, without
much regard to the particular type of government or the
merits of the existing regime, because they saw the only alternative to be a bloodbath. During the Biafran war "the
Pope expressed the belief that a federally imposed military
solution was impossible because 'protracted war would
either lead to foreign intervention or a permanent split of
Nigeria.' A compromise, he suggested, was the best alternative" (Stremlau 1977, p. 345). More frequently, the change
in attitudes must be both produced and recognized by the
parties themselves. Before they moved to a negotiated
compromise—withdrawal of missiles in exchange for a
pledge not to invade—President Kennedy and Premier
Khrushchev had to convince themselves and each other
that the only alternative was nuclear war (Snyder 1978, pp
358f).

Another type of perceived change concerns power relations, including such items as stalemate and equality.

> The moment is propitious for negotiation when power re-
> lations shift toward equality: when the former upper
> hand slips, or the former underdog improves his posi-
> tion.

When the formerly dominant party loses its exclusive
control over the problem, it may want to put all its efforts

into reasserting its predominance, to be sure, but it may also come to realize that it is better to talk now while it is still in a relatively favorable position than continue to hold out and face an even worse moment. Here the role of warnings is important, for the party must be convinced that in fact things will continue to get worse.

Similarly, when the formerly excluded party is able to show some increase in its power, although it may thus find encouragement to continue its struggle until the tables are completely turned, it is more likely to be satisfied by the recognition of its improved position signaled by the other party's agreement to begin negotiations. It is true that the situations are not symmetrical: In the first case the party losing its dominant position must be convinced that things will continue to get worse; whereas in the second case the formerly excluded party must be convinced that things will not get much better soon. But then people do not always arrive at the same decision for the same reasons.

The recognition of these two effects is a nutshell description of the whole strategy of negotiations for the independence of colonies; the metropole negotiated independence when it felt the wave of history was no longer with it and it had to try to salvage what it could of the situation, and the nationalists negotiated after some significant victories—electoral or guerrilla—raised their status, even though the wave of history was with them. The case of Zimbabwe, cited above, is only the most recent example of this effect. It applies also to the October 1973 war in the Middle East, a situation which—for all the criticisms of his particular role—Kissinger perceived most accurately: Egypt was buoyed enough by its initial performance and the erasure of the myth of the easily defeated Arabs to be ready to talk, and Israel had enough of the cockiness knocked out of it to be willing to talk too. A destruction of the Egyptian Third Army west of the canal would have destroyed these changes and restored the unwillingness of both parties to negotiate just as would a total Israeli defeat.

A similar situation had occurred to a lesser degree in 1970, when the newly acquired Russian arms buoyed the Arabs' spirit and gave pause to the dominant Israelis; the effect was not great enough on its own nor was it effectively used by third parties, however, to produce negotiations on any goal higher than ending the war of attrition. Similarly, the Lebanese civil war of 1976 helped contribute to the balance of forces propitious for negotiation, particularly in its weakening effects on the Palestine parties. As Henry Tanner noted, "The willingness of the Palestinians to negotiate is the direct result of the loss they suffered in the Lebanese war. 'We have no choice but to fit ourselves into the Arab context now, and the Arabs want to negotiate,' a Fatah official said" (*New York Times*, December 10, 1976). But the effect did not operate on both sides, and the negotiations had to wait a full year before being reinvigorated without the Palestine Liberation Organization (PLO).

In the third quarter of this century the bargaining positions of the Organization of Petroleum Exporting Countries (OPEC) and the major international oil companies were nearly reversed. In the early 1950s, the oil companies could use the threat to cut production in one country and to increase it in another as a weapon against an uncompliant country. By 1970, when membership in OPEC united the policies and bargaining positions of oil-producing nations, it was made clear to the oil companies that if negotiations deadlocked with one country the companies would not be allowed to increase production elsewhere but instead stood in danger of a total embargo on their operations. In September 1970, Colonel Quaddafi of Libya exploited the conjunction of the increase in demand and expected decrease in supply to show both OPEC governments and the oil companies that the power relationship of the two groups had been reversed. Negotiations were never the same again once Qaddafi demonstrated how effectively production cuts and threats of shutdowns could be used against individual companies (see Rustow 1976, pp. 20–21; Schuler 1976). The Indonesian Minister of Basic Industries and Mines expressed his idea of the new relationship sought, not only in the petroleum market but in the whole new international economic order: "We are willing to cooperate with everybody, but with cooperation as two equal partners. For this we have a saying in our language: '*duduk sama rendah, berdiri sama tinggi*,' roughly translated, 'we need them as partners, not as leeches' " (Kubbah 1974, p. 106).

These examples show that the change in relative power is as much a matter of perception as of material fortunes. "Feeling more equal," losing the stigma of being a pushover, getting one's comeuppance (even if battlelines are not materially changed) are all often as important as actually equalizing power or its sources or even of winning a crucial battle. U.N. resolutions, governments-in-exile, and foreign visits are sometimes the symbolic equivalents of more substantial power equalizers.

To Overcome the Double Veto

Negotiation is appropriate when all parties to the dispute have a veto over its solution.

While this is the clearest way of putting it, there are other ways of saying the same thing: Negotiation is necessary to solve a problem when both parties are equal, when each party has the power to block the other's attainment of its goal, or when both parties' agreement is needed for a solution.

These different formulations point up the fact that negotiations arise from a double veto, when both parties can block a negotiated solution if it does not satisfy them, but can also prevent a unilateral solution from taking place if it excludes them. This is a profound expression of the equality of the parties in negotiation (as already noted in regard to the decision rule), although of course it does not mean that all parties must be equal in all aspects. Parties then come to view the ability of the other side to block a solution as reason to come to terms. The Israelis have long refused to negotiate with the Palestinians, who they said did not constitute a legitimate negotiating entity. The Egyptian president, however, made it clear in all his public statements that there could be no comprehensive solution of the Middle East situation without the Palestinians, and the PLO has continually sought to convey the idea that no solution was possible without it.

Sir Geoffrey Harrison, the British representative in talks on the issue of Trieste, saw the Yugoslavs and Italians, who blocked each other's claim to territory in the area between them, move in the direction of negotiations. "They both claimed to have rights to more territory. They both knew they could not get it. They both realized that the best they could hope to get was Zone A and Zone B, respectively. So they decided with reason and logic, I think, they had better make the best of it and get a settlement" (Campbell 1976, pp. 72–73).

On the other hand, the refusal of one side to admit the equality of the other is frequently a major obstacle to negotiation. This is another expression of the subjectiveness of obstacles, although the refusing party almost always claims that it is referring to an objective situation of fact or at least of right, not merely to a perception. Again, the United States and the Vietcong, France and the FLN, the Greek and Turkish Cypriots, and the Egyptians and Israelis long refused to recognize the equal right and power of the other side to participate in determining a solution to their common problem. The recognition that no solution was possible without the participation of the other party, whose interests therefore had to be satisfied to some extent by it, was in each case a crucial element in the decision to explore the possibility of negotiations. It may take a long time for the issue to ripen to the point where this mutual veto power is recognized by both sides, or it can happen suddenly and dramatically. Yet it is not the issue alone which changes or ripens, but rather the relationship of the parties which is being tested and reinforced. During this time, each party—or at least the party being challenged—will try to show that it has the power or the right to impose a unilateral solution to the problem, in effect to show that the other party's presumed veto is inoperative. Only when both sides recognize that the issue can only be resolved by a joint decision can the search for that solution—that is, the negotiation process—be begun.

The Rhodesian situation is a case in point. Only when both parties agreed that the other was necessary to a solution could negotiations take place. In 1976 and before, it was Smith's government that was being pressed to recognize the right and power of the Zimbabwe nationalists to join in determining the shape of the future government. But when Smith effectively denied this right, the nationalist Patriotic Front decided to increase its power, and it became the Zimbabweans who had to be persuaded of the right and power of the Smith regime to claim a role in determining the next regime, and hence of the appropriateness of negotiation at all. When the new British Conservative government threatened to strengthen the Smith–Muzorewa regime with recognition, and the latter had inflicted heavy damage on the Patriotic Front's sanctuary states on the front line but still not enough damage to reverse the tide of history and win the war, the mutual ability of both sides to impose a veto on the other's solution was finally recognized and negotiations leading to the Lancaster House Agreement of 1979 were possible. Negotiation is truly an event to be seized at the proper moment, lest the forces that led to that moment continue to act and cause the moment to pass.

So too with the case of the Paris negotiations on Vietnam, which could not begin until the fall of 1972, when both parties finally realized that neither could settle the situation unilaterally, so they needed to make a joint decision on the future. When the mutual veto was recognized, negotiations could begin.

Nasser claimed that his nationalization of the Suez Canal Company in 1956 was within Egypt's legal rights and hence not a matter for negotiation. He refused to attend the London Conference of twenty-two nations but did agree to receive the Menzies Committee in Cairo. In his memoirs, Sir Anthony Eden gives a substantially verbatim account of discussions between Nasser and Menzies:

> *Menzies:* What you are overlooking is that the actual thing you did was to repudiate (and I use that expression because plain language will be appreciated) a concession which had twelve years to run.
>
> *Nasser:* But how could anybody complain about that if it was within our power?
>
> *Menzies:* I don't concede it was within your power. In fact I think it was not. But can't you see that if your attitude is that merely because it was within your power you can repudiate a contract binding upon you, this, in one hit, destroys the confidence that the world has in your contractual word?
>
> *Nasser:* I don't understand this. The concession would have expired in twelve years anyhow and then I suppose the same uproar would have occurred, if you are right.
>
> *Menzies:* Not at all. If you had not interfered with the concession, I have no doubt that the company itself would have quite soon begun negotiations with you for

some future organization for the canal. But those negotiations would have been conducted in an atmosphere which was not one of crisis, and sensible and fair conclusions might well have been arrived at without the heated exchanges on such matters as "sovereignty."

Nasser: But this ignores the fact that we had the right to do what we did, and if we have the right to do something we can't understand how people can take exception to it. (Eden, pp. 526–27)

In this instance, as long as Nasser refused to admit that the canal stockholders or users had any right or ability to contest his decision, there was no recognition of a mutual veto and no opportunity for negotiation.

It is important here to avoid the notion that negotiation is "the good thing" because we are writing about it, and that all other ways of arriving at a solution are evil. It is quite natural, wherever possible, for each party to try to avoid sharing the decision-making with its opponent and to escape the opponent's veto attempts. The examples of joint or negotiated decisions where unilateral solutions proved impossible—examples such as Vietnam, Algeria, Cyprus, and Sinai, among others—should not hide the many other cases where a challenging party tried to impose its right to participate in the solution of a problem and was defeated in the attempt, as the Suez example shows. The stalemate of 1917 in World War I gave way to the Allied victory of 1918 which left little room for negotiation; the negotiation feelers from the Axis toward the end of World War II were rejected by the Allies who wanted unconditional, not negotiated, surrender. Plenty of unilateral decisions are made each day at all levels where other parties would like to participate but are unable to impose the stalemate that would give them the power to do so. So it is not surprising that the decision to explore the possibility of negotiations may be slow in coming on a given issue and, even once negotiation has begun, each party may well be constantly alert to the possibility of escaping the other's veto and resolving the issue on its own.

Furthermore, there are other reasons besides winning for a party to want to avoid negotiation. It may want to look tough for a home audience, for example, or to draw attention from other problems, or to impose the hardship of a festering conflict on the enemy, or to make propaganda. In all these cases, the conflict simply does not hurt the party enough— either relative to its own security point or to the discomfort imposed on the other party—to persuade it to negotiate.

To Create New Outcomes

Negotiations are appropriate when they deal with a new outcome that can be created only jointly.

This new "good" that negotiation can bring about can be a positive creation—such as the steel that results from negotiating the terms on which coal and iron are brought together in an industrial common market—or it can be the end of an intolerable situation—such as the termination of war by negotiating the terms of a peace treaty. In either case, the goal is not unilaterally attainable and therefore requires the joint decision that is arrived at through negotiation. In the process, negotiation is used both to create the new good and to decide on the allocation of shares in it; these shares are the terms on which the decision is made. It is as if the agreement created a fund out of which the parties agreed to pay themselves for concluding the agreement. Parties deciding to establish peace also decide on the allocation of benefits from it, much as parties deciding to create a steel company decide on the contributions, benefits, and rules for future determination of these ingredients. It is this jointly determined allocation which tells each party whether its participation in creating the new outcome is worth it or not.

"Worth it" has to be judged against two imaginary reference points that a negotiator must constantly keep in mind. One is his *expected outcome,* the maximum that he feels he can realistically obtain from the other party. If this optimal point is lower than the contributions he is required to make to obtain an agreement, the outcome is not worth the effort to him. The other point is his *security position,* his estimate of the costs and benefits he would encounter without an agreement. Again, if this point is scarcely less favorable than the expected outcome or the current offers, he will be less interested in an agreement than if his security position is quite painful and unacceptable. In the words of Livingston Merchant, who had a long and distinguished career in the United States Foreign Service, "The objective of any successful negotiator is knowing in advance what the absolute minimum is that you can accept, and where you are prepared to walk out and have the negotiation fail completely if you can't maintain your minimum position" (Merchant interview).

Secretary Kissinger made specific use of these concepts in trying to sell the idea of a Golan Heights disengagement to Israel in 1974.

> Israel does not have a choice between a good alternative and a bad one but between two bad ones. The first [security position] is to remain stubborn, allowing the negotiations to fail with all the consequences for relations with the United States. The second alternative [expected outcome]—territorial concessions with a security risk. What is preferable? This unfortunately can be known only after the fact. (Golan 1976, p. 190)

One important lesson the Israelis learned after the 1973 war in the Middle East, according to Safran, is that even a militarily weaker opponent may choose to go to war if left with no better options: "Israelis had deemed war 'impossible' because they thought Sadat would not possibly hope to win. They did not realize that it might pay him to go to war if he had reasonable chances of not suffering a crushing defeat very quickly" (Safran 1974, p. 230). Thus, "worth it" decision-making also takes into account estimates of the other side's thinking.

It is evident that these terms are shorthand for a complex aggregate of ingredients and it would be unrealistic as well as difficult to try to arrive at a single, quantitative figure for these "points." Nevertheless, they represent concepts that the negotiator has to keep in mind as he asks himself "whether an agreement is worth it at this point," just as he might ask himself whether it was worthwhile going to the office this Saturday morning, that is, whether there was enough to be accomplished to justify the inconvenience of travel and the opportunities lost for doing other things. The Saturday morning decision is a unilateral one (in principle), whereas the negotiated decision is bilateral since it involves a good that is jointly created.

There may be no single outcome that both parties prefer to lack of agreement, or, as Ambassador Kenneth Rush stated it, "situations where a negotiation is utterly impossible, in which case it will break down very soon. . . . If they [the parties' objectives] are completely incompatible you might as well face up to it. An agreement that ignores that incompatibility is not going to be a worthwhile agreement" (Rush interview). Unless new objectives are made to emerge, either through reassessment of the current "worth its" or creation of new outcomes, the negotiations will fail (Sawyer and Guetzkow 1965, p. 485). The decision of each party to try to negotiate involves an evaluation of possible outcomes to determine whether the outcome created—and each party's share of it—justifies the cost involved.

To Set the Terms of Trade

Negotiations are also appropriate when they deal with an exchange of outcomes that can only be decided upon jointly.

In the previous case, the new outcome was shared; in this case new outcomes are traded. In this sense, negotiation is the means of establishing terms of trade in a contract when the values or "prices" of the exchanged items are not fixed. The reasoning of the parties is the same as in any prospective purchasing—or more appropriately, barter—situation. A party wants the other party to give up something and looks about for an acceptable item of exchange, or a party wants to give up something that is valued by the other and tries to establish a fair price in some currency the first party values. Often this "something" is simply a veto on an acceptable resolution of the problem at hand, and the first party has to come up with an appropriate item of exchange for the other party to remove its veto and lift the stalemate. Unusual though it may seem, this type of image can be used in many situations to show the appropriateness of negotiation for solving the problem and to show the degree of exchange required for a joint decision. Thus, the Zimbabwe nationalists in 1977–78 were trying to buy into Rhodesian government—indeed, to buy a controlling share—while at the same time employing guerrilla warfare to render impossible or to veto the normal function of that government in the absence of their participation; the Rhodesian government, in turn, was seeking to buy off that veto—if it could not otherwise remove it—and the only acceptable coin for the nationalists was participation. This exchange—recognition of each other's right to participate—was the basis of the Lancaster House Agreement of December 1979. In the disengagement rounds the Israelis had a saying, "The depth of the retreat depends on the size of the compensation" (Allon in Golan 1976, p. 222). Any negotiation is a matter of each side's establishing how much it wants and how much it is willing to give to get it, and then bringing the two into balance. Even when preparing its first series of options for consideration in SALT, the American side sought to establish a basic exchange of desiderata with the Russians. "In return for indulging Moscow's preference on ABM, Washington hoped to gain what it wanted most: a ceiling on the Soviet offensive missile program. . . . " This is essentially what happened in the end, although it took a while to get there. This statement is a good example of Homans's maxim discussed in chapter 1.

Necessary and Sufficient Conditions

All of these different ways of characterizing appropriate situations for negotiation can be summarized by saying that negotiation is appropriate when the parties see that a problem can only be resolved jointly and when they have the will to end an existing situation that they consider unacceptable, while admitting the other party's or parties' claim to participate in that solution. Perception, will, and equality—of these three, the most important of all is will. Without the will to reach agreement there will be none, even if the other party's claim to participate in a solution is admitted.

Ernst van der Beugel, who represented the Netherlands in the Common Market negotiations, recalled de Gaulle's lack of willingness to see the negotiations over Britain's entry into the European Community succeed in 1961–62:

> I don't think that anybody really knew—we had our doubts and so on—but there was no consensus whatsoever as to whether the French were totally disinterested in the details of the negotiations because they knew the General at a certain moment would say no anyhow, or whether the negotiations could have succeeded. Now in hindsight it is quite clear that if the British had given *everything* the General would still have said no. (van der Beugel interview)

After the third round of meetings of the Eighteen-Nation Disarmament Conference in Geneva in the early sixties, the nonaligned nations that participated in the talks reported back to the General Assembly that, if there was no agreement, "it was for the lack of political will on the part of the nuclear powers and not for any dearth of fresh ideas" (Ahmed 1967, p. 17). The nuclear powers may have seen different reasons for non-agreement, but nevertheless without the will to agree, for reasons deemed subjective or objective, there will be no agreement. The classic example is the Austrian Peace Treaty, which was simply impossible to attain as long as the will to negotiate was negated by Stalin but was quite conceivable as soon as that will could exist.

But will, perception, and equality apply to a number of specific elements, such as the unacceptability of the situation, inability to improve the situation alone, and acceptance of the other party. Clearly, these items are related and even sequential. Probably the first condition is realization that the situation is unacceptable, either because it is intolerably costly or because, intolerable or not, it can be improved. Many observers of the dramatic events in the Middle East in late 1977 pointed to the growing price of non-agreement for Egypt. With domestic economic woes and Soviet-made equipment soon to be without spare parts, Egypt, in the view of many, could not afford to have the state of belligerence with Israel continue. It is not surprising that President Sadat's initiative took place in the same year as the January 1977 riots protesting the removal of price subsidies in Egypt.

Sometimes the realization that a situation can go on no longer is imposed from the outside. In the case of Trieste, negotiations were triggered by an action which demonstrated that doing nothing to resolve the problem could lead to active military hostilities. When the two occupying countries, the United States and Great Britain, announced on October 8, 1953, that they planned to turn over the governing authority of one of the two zones to Italy, which in effect would have split the territory along occupation lines, there was tremendous opposition, both popular and governmental, in Yugoslavia. The Yugoslav negotiator, Vladimir Velebit, recounted, "When we understood that you, the Americans and British, were a hundred percent serious in wanting to withdraw the troops at the earliest possibility, then we knew there was no more playing around; we had to find a solution" (Campbell 1976, p. 98).

At other times the parties impose the unacceptable situation on each other, not necessarily simultaneously. The Tet offensive of 1968 and the bombings and minings of the North in 1972 brought home this fact to the United States and to North Vietnam, respectively, four years apart. The Forest Hills, New York, confrontation in 1972 over a low-income housing project in a middle-class neighborhood opened to compromise and negotiation when the opponents came to see that total opposition was doomed to total defeat. "They realize that if there is no compromise the original project will be built" said Mayor Lindsay's mediator, Mario Cuomo, before recommending modifications in the project (*New York Times*, July 15, 1972).

The second condition is the realization that this unacceptability cannot be corrected alone or, as psychologists call it, the recognition of superordinate goals—those "which are compelling for all and cannot be ignored, but which cannot be achieved by the efforts and resources of one group alone. They require the coordinated efforts and resources of the groups involved" (Sherif 1962, p. 11). Both of these conditions—unacceptability and insufficiency—are matters of sliding costs and benefits or of relative judgment. They generally mean that at a given level of expectations and efforts it may be possible to improve the situation, but only in conjunction with another party that has a stake in the results.

While the nature of this condition will be developed further later on, it does serve here to introduce the third condition: the participation of the other party or the acceptance of its claim to some benefits. This is, in many cases, a major stumbling block, for it involves judgments on legitimacy that the contesting party often seeks to deny. These three conditions, then, add up to a perception of negotiability and a will to negotiate, the basic ingredients in the decision to explore the possibility of negotiating.

CREATING OPPORTUNITIES

The preceding attempt to identify potentially negotiable issues has not been simply an exercise in classification. Since these characteristics are subjective matters of perception and will, they can be manipulated. Rarely do both parties arrive at the decision to explore the possibility of negotiation at the same time, so it becomes important to the first to do so to be able to influence the other's decision in the same direction. The paradox of this situation is that, to the party which has not (yet) decided to negotiate, the decision of the other party is a prima facie reason for the first to continue to refuse because it makes it appear that the other party is yielding. If the first party can only hold out a little longer, the other might give in completely. The decision to negotiate is seen both as a claim to participate in the solution of the issue, which is not recognized by the non-negotiator, and as a sign of weakness, since the negotiator is now willing to compromise. It is against such renewed obstacles that one party must try to create or reinforce the conditions that justify negotiation in the other's eyes.

In his memoirs, Anthony Eden describes the circumstances that led to the opening of the Geneva Conference on Indochina in 1954. In preparing for a meeting with Chou En-lai, Eden needed to determine whether the Chinese government was prepared to come to an arrangement at all and to determine if, in Chinese eyes, the conditions existed to justify a negotiation:

> The French could still hold onto Indo-China but at any moment some major disaster might overcome them and

no choice be left but an ignominious exodus. While the French armies were still in being, we had a certain bargaining factor, weak though it was. With every month that passed this counted for less. . . . If we could not reach agreement soon, the military position would deteriorate and it would then become evident to the world that the Chinese had no need to bargain. The Chinese themselves probably knew this already, but they might be wise enough to reckon that it was not good politics to drive an enemy to despair. In a few months' time nothing but capitulation would suffice. The question was whether the Chinese saw matters in this light. (Eden 1960, pp. 138–39)

Creating Solutions

The most positive way of bringing about negotiations is to *show the other party the possibilities of creative solutions*. J. Robert Schaetzel, a seasoned U.S. diplomat, described international negotiations as "a set of common problems to which the answers are very difficult to find, and hopefully they will come out of the common search. I think we have lost great ground in recent years by transferring so many problems from this framework into those which are really looked upon as adversary relationships in which there are sharply conflicting interests and somebody has got to win, somebody has got to lose" (Schaetzel interview). This approach can take a number of forms.

New solutions, new alternatives, new ways of defining the issue, new possibilities for flexibility can be suggested, to *show that the parties are not locked in their stalemate* but can get out of their impasse with a show of creative goodwill. Creative problem-solving can be illustrated by the dispute between two people over whether a window should be opened or closed. As long as they continue to argue on that basis, one will win and one will lose. But if they can restate the issue to show that what one really wants is to have fresh air and the other to avoid a draft, then they can open a window in an adjacent room and the door in between and both can "win" by participating in a creative solution (Follett 1951, p. 118). In the same way, if one party can suggest alternative solutions to more serious international problems, then it may be possible to bring about negotiations.

The initiating party has to be careful not to get locked into specific proposals at this point, but rather to make it understood that the solutions, alternatives, definitions, and possibilities are cited merely as examples of the type of outcome that might be possible. For this purpose, unofficial statements, personal views, private articles, and other trial balloons are useful. Ambiguity plays a large part in the prenegotiation stage. Too much clarity before a position has been jointly defined between parties may make concessions difficult when negotiations begin, and ambiguity may provide flexibility in a prenegotiatory period. Even more important than ambiguity, for the same reasons, is avoidance of binding commitment. The prenegotiatory period is a time to probe and explore, and to show the other side examples of possibilities, but not a time to make specific promises. Kissinger's efforts from as early as 1968 focused on getting Hanoi to indicate "the kinds of outcomes" that it could accept in line with its goals, and after 1970 he tried to show Hanoi "the kinds of outcomes" the United States could offer.

After the first meeting of Prime Minister Begin and President Sadat of Egypt in late 1977, both leaders publicly announced their agreement on the fact that "everything is negotiable but the destruction of the State of Israel." Before the negotiating meetings opened on January 10, however, there was a hardening of attitudes on both sides. Both parties were making public statements about their conditions for a settlement. The rhetoric became so inflammatory that the

United States tried to convince the parties to keep a lid on public statements. The meetings in Jerusalem recessed shortly after they opened, both sides accusing each other of setting impossible terms.

Another way of showing the possibilities for creative solutions is to suggest the possibility of exchanges, side-payments, compensation, and other contingent benefits as inducement for agreement. The possibility that one party is looking for exchanges rather than simply expecting the other party to give in may be enough to draw the other party into negotiation. Again, however, the initiator must be careful not to present his suggestions as if they were precise proposals. This mistake has been made on occasion in advance of American base negotiations in various countries (Spain, Philippines) when the idea of aid "to pay" for use of the facilities has been advanced and then taken for granted. Generally, it is the idea that a particular good is available for exchange against another item—such as the Israelis letting it be known that they would trade territory for the end of war—that is put forward, leaving the quantity of each good to be exchanged to be worked out in the negotiations. Kissinger probably made more consistent use of side-payments to buy an agreement than most other secretaries of state—in the Vietnam agreement, in the second Sinai disengagement agreement, in the maritime International Enterprise to be created by the Law of the Sea, in the Philippine base negotiations, and in the Rhodesian transition proposals, large amounts of money and other things were pledged in order to gain agreement. Sometimes it worked.

A third way is to show that a new good might be created by joint action where it could never exist by unilateral decision. The initiator must show how the other party stands to gain from the new creation, without hiding the fact that the initiator too will benefit; too great a gain for the second party will arouse his suspicions, whereas too great a gain for the initiator will not attract the other party. Here again, it is the idea of jointly created gain that is suggested in order to bring about a decision to negotiate, with the negotiations themselves covering the allocation of contributions and benefits.

These kinds of proposals are positive exercises of power, designed to suggest gratifications to the other side contingent on its agreement to negotiate. These gratifications may be provided by the initiating party—as in the case of the new alternatives and the exchanges—or the initiator may merely be pointing out that they will accrue to participants by the nature of things, as in the case of newly created goods. In the first case, such an exercise of power is a *promise* (or "volitional gratification"), and in the second, a *prediction* (or "non-volitional gratification"). This distinction will come up again when the negotiations actually begin.

Promises and predictions were paired with their negative counterparts—threats and warnings, discussed in the next section—to make up the core of President Carter's speech of July 21, 1977, an important ingredient in the SALT II negotiations:

> Our cruise missiles are aimed at compensating for the growing threat to our deterrent capability represented by the buildup of Soviet strategic offensive weapons forces. If these threats can be controlled, we are prepared to limit our own strategic programs. [Promise]
> But if an agreement cannot be reached, there should be no doubt that the United States can and will do what it must to protect its security and insure the adequacy of its strategic posture. [Threat]
> Our view is that a SALT agreement which just reflects the lowest common denominator that can be agreed upon will only create an illusion of progress and, eventually, a backlash against the entire arms control process. (Warning) Our view is that genuine progress in SALT will not

merely stabilize competition in weapons but can also provide a basis for improvement in political relations. [Prediction]

Avoiding Disaster

As the other side of the coin, negotiations can be brought about by convincing the other party that only worse alternatives exist in the absence of a joint solution. By showing that a stalemate does exist, that there is no way out in the absence of talks, or that things will (or can be made to) get worse as time goes on without a settlement, the party is able to put teeth in its demand for negotiations.

By the late 1950s it was apparent that the situation in the Antarctic was becoming increasingly dangerous. There were no limits on research, and several nations claimed the territory and the right to conduct unlimited research with no restrictions on peaceful or nonpeaceful activities. In 1958 President Eisenhower invited the states with claims in the area and eleven other nations engaged in the International Geophysical Year activities to participate in a conference to keep Antarctica "from becoming an object of political conflict" and to keep it an area "open to all nations to conduct scientific or other peaceful activities." The conference ultimately produced a treaty that internationalized and demilitarized the continent (see Taubenfeld 1961, pp. 273–74), thus averting potential risks recognized by many countries.

In 1974 Acting President Glafkos Clerides of Cyprus tried to convince legal but deposed President Makarios of the need to accept "geographical federation" as a basis for negotiations with the occupying Turks. Clerides felt that the alternative to acceptance of the formula was no agreement at all and the incorporation of northern Cyprus as a Turkish colony. The question, as Clerides put it, was whether Makarios "is ready to face reality," to which a Greek-Cypriot source answered, "I think the Archbishop sees the reality but

I'm not sure he's ready to acknowledge what he sees"—a perceptive analysis of objective and subjective ingredients. In fact, Makarios was not able to come to terms with reality and northern Cyprus became a Turkish colony for the rest of the decade (*New York Times*, December 4, 1974).

Worse alternatives can be suggested in two ways, by threats and by warnings. Both are forecasts of disaster to come, the threat referring to a deprivation that a party imposes by its own will and the *warning* referring to a calamity that will take place independent of any human agent. In both cases, the future disaster is posed as an alternative to negotiation, making the latter look beneficial by comparison. Warnings are safer to use, since the parties then have a good reason to unite and work together to avoid impending catastrophe, whereas threats create contradictory feelings: the other party is repelled by the threat that is supposed to attract him to negotiate a joint agreement. Threats, like vetos, have a way of creating opposition rather than progress toward negotiations, becoming the issue themselves rather than drawing attention to the original stalemate to be overcome. Diplomats usually echo the words of de Gaulle that they will not negotiate under pressure or be brought to the negotiating table by force. As the North Vietnamese often proclaimed, they would not be bombed to the table. But since parties will frequently not negotiate in the absence of pressure either, the question becomes which form of pressure is the most conducive to negotiation. Warnings, like stalemates, are theoretically better, if feasible, but sometimes threats are required.

Kissinger warned the Law of the Sea Conference in 1976 that the next administration would be no easier to deal with (while at the same time promising financial support for the proposed international mining agency). He also threatened to go it alone if the others did not reach an acceptable agreement. "We do not like being bullied," one delegate replied and the conference bogged down. President Carter six months later threatened—the newspapers wrote "warned," to sidestep the unpleasant connotations of "threatened"—to consider acceleration of American weapons development if the Russians failed to negotiate seriously about arms control. Both efforts to show a worse alternative failed. On the other hand, Panamanian authorities and many Americans warned for a long time that the situation within Panama was potentially explosive, with dire consequences for America's ability to keep the canal open, unless a new treaty were negotiated. These warnings went on for so long that they were almost like crying "Wolf!", but they eventually had an effect.

Unlike the positive approach previously mentioned, the negative approach usually cannot be made effective by words alone; often some illustrative action or down payment on the threat or warning is needed to bring home the notion that without negotiations things will be worse or at least no better. Threats and warnings have to be made credible, and they have to be protected against countertactics—"You can't do that! You wouldn't do that! It won't happen!" Thus there is pressure, particularly on the threatener, to show that he can and will carry out his threat.

The East Germans and the Soviet Union did not want the West to renew the viability of the West German currency in the early 1950s. To prevent this action they initiated the Berlin blockade—a threatening gesture designed to ward off any such action. Robert Lovett, who was involved in U.S. policymaking to deal with the threat, recalled why the attempt to cut off West Berlin failed:

I knew from experience [when I was] in charge of all Air Forces during the war that we had lifted 72,000 tons over the Himalayas. . . . Therefore the thing to do is to break the blockade. Don't get frightened about it. If they shoot

down one of our planes they are at war because they have
no right to air corridors. As soon as they saw that we were
putting in all the food, coal, and flour that was needed to
keep Berlin alive, there went the ballgame. Right there
and then we renewed the viability of the currency.
(Lovett interview)

Threatening action can take a number of forms, each with
its problems. Most basic are the stalemate and the veto.
"Stalemate" exists when the circumstances prevent either
party from creating a solution alone. Each party has necessary but insufficient ingredients of a solution; making this
fact known to another party in the same position (assuming
that together their ingredients are sufficient) can turn stalemate into agreement.

"Veto" is used here to refer to a situation in which each
party can prevent the other from creating a solution. The
need to make the other party recognize that it is part of the
problem and therefore must be part of the solution is the im-
pelling force behind wars and rebellions for negotiated
goals. Such action as a tactic to bring about negotiations carries with it the danger that the other party may try to remove
the veto by removing the vetoer, and the whole topic of
negotiations disappears in the smoke. Nationalist movements veto the efforts of colonial governments to restore law
and order without them. If they survive attempts to eliminate
them—and their record is rather good—they become part of
a stalemate and then of the solution, after having been part of
the problem.

As with promises and predictions, and threats and
warnings, discussed above, the distinction is between volitional and nonvolitional types of power. Stalemate is better
as a tactic than veto; it is less vulnerable, less likely to become an issue or subject of attack itself, and it is friendlier. A
stalemate is not always obvious, however; the other party

often thinks it can do it alone (even though it does not appear to be very successful at doing it), and if it notices the party that wants negotiation at all, sees its actions as willful veto. Nuclear disarmament is an example of a stalemate situation—like marriage, it is impossible to achieve unilaterally, and parties are continually telling each other that unless the other takes up the offers of mutual arms control, the situation will both voluntarily and automatically get worse for both.

Bowing to External Pressure

A third way to bring about negotiations—a special case of the second—is to bow before external pressure from a third party. Since such pressure works best when it is perceived as being neutral as well as inescapable, the party using a third party to bring pressure to bear must be subtle and indirect in its own role, lest the third party be perceived as merely an agent of the first. Of course, nothing requires the third party itself to be subtle and indirect, except for the general requirements of effectiveness. The third party can in turn use the kinds of tactics spelled out above: pointing out benefits that will flow from a solution or new possibilities for resolving the problem, showing harm that will occur if no solution is found, or even taking on a more active role and offering inducements for a negotiated outcome or threatening deprivations if one or both parties refuse to talk. Secretary of State Kissinger used all these devices on his shuttle visits between Egypt and Israel following the June 1973 war in the Middle East. Great Britain did too in bringing Rhodesians and Zimbabweans to an agreement in 1979, after previous failures by the British and the Americans; Lord Carrington was able to threaten the Patriotic Front with ultimatums to proceed without them at a number of crucial stages. Nationalist movements have often had the force of the United Nations enlisted on their behalf to bring about negotiations, but it is rarely effective because it is too closely associated with one side and not enough of a "third" party. Third-party pressure can be very effective, however, when it comes from some institutionalized moral force, a joint patron of the two parties, or a collective body of friends and peers, all of whom can exert some moral pressure on the parties.

One recent agreement that was reached with third-party pressure concerned the Ganges River dispute between India and Bangladesh. During the dry season there is insufficient water to supply both countries, and claims and counterclaims were traded concerning India's construction of a dam diverting water from Bangladesh. Bangladesh brought the dispute to the fall 1976 session of the Special Political Committee in an attempt to involve the United Nations. With the help of third parties from the nonaligned group of which both parties are members, a "consensual statement" was worked out behind the scenes. The two parties agreed to resume bilateral talks in Dacca in December, which ultimately produced a formal agreement. The agreement to resume talks avoided a vote in the United Nations in which member states would have had to choose between the claims of the two states. The pressure of the nonaligned third parties was strengthened by the known opposition of the group to outside interference—and especially big power involvement—in problems arising between members of the group (see Hertz 1977).

Similarly, the Organization for African Unity has been effective in bringing its members out of confrontation and into negotiation, primarily by admonition but also because the attention of the international organization means that hitherto neglected grievances at least get a hearing. Analyzing the tactics of third parties is complex, because they can occupy a wide variety of positions ranging from completely disinterested third party to third party with direct interests in the conflict, including shared interests with one of the sides. They will not be examined here since other works address the subject (see Edmead 1971, Fisher 1978, Rubin 1981).

Narrowing Differences

A final way of bringing about negotiations is to *show the amount of agreement that exists and narrow the subjects of disagreement.* In this case, the perception of the other party is manipulated by showing him the many—even if minor— areas of agreement and by isolating the few—albeit major— areas of disagreement. Drawing up such a balance sheet has the advantage of putting the various issues into perspective, but it has the further effect of getting the parties to start communicating and exchanging ideas about the general problem.

George McGhee, then Under-Secretary for Political Affairs, was sent to the Congo during the secession of Katanga province to talk to the secessionist leader, Moise Tshombe, about accepting the U.N. plan to deal with the conflict.

> My deliberate tactic, knowing that I couldn't get everything I wanted from him to carry out the U Thant plan, was to see how much I could get from him that was consistent with the plan. He would at least be headed in the direction of the plan. . . . Well, he ended up agreeing to about four or five very concrete steps, which were movements forward and announced publicly that he would carry them out unilaterally. (McGhee interview)

By looking for areas where agreement already exists, the parties may find that less separates them than they thought; they may also discover that the gap is greater, but at least they have begun provisionally the negotiating process. Usually in the process they will want to establish a third category of issues, where neither agreement nor disagreement will be established for the moment, the parties reserving these items for possible bargaining when the topics of disagreement are discussed. This type of inducement to negotiate is usually possible only when regular contacts—ambassadors, or delegations to the same international organization such as the United Nations or a regional body—already function and representatives can meet and discuss without a specific decision to start negotiating. Much can be accomplished in these sounding stages.

BEHAVIOR IN THE PRENEGOTIATION PERIOD: A SUMMARY

The tactics suggested above are not piano keys, which, when pressed, bring forth an immediate sound. They often cover years of effort, between the time when one party decides that the problem is appropriate for negotiation and the time when it convinces the other party. They generally require a great deal of time: first in implementing, then in communicating to the other party, and then still more time for the trial and error process of thinking up new alternatives and communicating them in turn. In the meantime, issues may move from front to back burner, as they heat up and cool down. In the latter periods, when other issues seem more pressing, less attention may be devoted to attempts to find some mutually acceptable solution, although in fact this would often be the best time to handle the problem, while it is not too hot. Issues do change as time passes, as often for the better as for the worse, and since there is no sure rule of thumb for distinguishing the conflicts that age well from those that age badly, there is no sound advice to be given about handling conflicts now rather than later. By the same token, many problems on the back burner never come forward again, at least in the same form, so that it is not clear that they even need handling when lukewarm. However, there are many identifiable situations when a dormant problem is sure enough to revive at some later date for efforts at problem-solving to be in order. Undelineated borders, unresolved issues from wartime, and many redistributive issues are good examples.

In general, the prenegotiation tactics can be summarized as attempts to show that a situation already painful in the absence of negotiations will become more so in the future, or that it can be improved through the mechanism of negotiations. Either external forces or willed acts of one party are invoked to strengthen the persuasion, and frequently the demonstration can be made credible only if the words are backed by a foretaste of things to come if negotiations do or do not take place.

There are a few dangers in this preliminary stage. One is that the means of pressure themselves may become the issue even before the real issue is met. Another is that the attempts to show that beneficial outcomes are possible through negotiation may so raise the expectations of the other party that it becomes insatiable when the talks actually begin. A third problem to avoid is the danger of premature proposals; this preliminary stage is not the time for concrete, official propositions, but for general ideas and trial balloons to identify the kind of things that might be possible if negotiations were ever to begin. Again, specific proposals might inflate expectations in the government or in domestic publics or might be judged on a take-it-or-leave-it basis as insufficient.

If successful, however, these tactics, and the realization of a negotiable situation on which they are based, may well bring the two parties to the point where they are willing to begin exploring the possibility of a negotiated solution. In the meantime, each party should be doing some serious studying and thinking, covering the items on the following checklist:

1. *Review and be well briefed in the facts of the problem, its cause, its history, its changes and evolution.*

Prenegotiation is a diagnostic phase where the nature of the conflict is thoroughly examined before remedies can be essayed. Facts include each party's position, which should be clearly and forcefully expressed.

2. *Look into precedents and referents governing similar situations.*

Are there established principles of justice dictating a particular outcome? Are there procedures for handling similar problems? Are there strong reasons for following or for avoiding these precedents?

3. *Know the contexts and perceptions that give meaning to the situation and its components.*

Obviously, in the strictest sense, this situation has never occurred before: In all other situations, something was different, if only (but usually a lot more than) the moment in time. It therefore becomes necessary to launch into the conceptual exercise (even if one does not use that term) of defining the type of situation and the type of events composing it. This search for the various definitions and referents of the problem is crucial to finding a solution and also to doing as much as possible toward making one's point of view prevail.

While the first two points—facts and precedents—speak for themselves, the search for definitions and referents is more complex. Yet there are plenty of examples. The Cuban missile crisis could be defined as an attempt by Cuba to defend itself, as an attempt by Russia to create a bargaining chip to trade for removal of U.S. missiles in Turkey, as an attempt by Russia to insure an American no-invasion pledge for Cuba, as an attempt by Russia to extend the territorial limits of its game preserve, or as a high-risk low-commitment move to test American responses and cop an advantage if possible. The two Shaba invasions of Zaire could be defined as tit-for-tat for Zaire's support of the UNITA rebels in Angola, a return of secessionist dissidents, the first move in a campaign to overthrow the Mobutu regime, or a Soviet thrust from radical Africa into moderate Africa. Since all of these are accurate, the way the situation is defined determines the way it will be handled and the degree to which it can be considered negotiable.

4. *Try to list and understand the stakes and interests of each side.*

This involves knowing what matters and what does not for oneself, separating the basic interests from the windfalls, dividing the negotiable from the non-negotiable elements, and also doing the same thing for the other side. It is especially important to be aware of the domestic and external pressures on negotiators of the other side. Writing on the day after the Egyptian–Israeli negotiations broke down on January 19, 1978, very soon after beginning, Henry Tanner commented in the *New York Times* that the Egyptians had underestimated the domestic political constraints on Begin—his cabinet, the political parties, and the public—while the Israelis seemed to show little understanding for Sadat's problems within the Arab world.

5. *Be aware of the affective elements in both parties' viewpoints of the situation, and of the emotional components of the other party.*

Issues of recognition, of dignity, of acceptance, of rights and justice may be more important than the actual disposition of a material good, and taking them into account may facilitate a solution. As Averell Harriman commented: "Instead of people going to extremes of trying to explain what 'nefarious plans' the other side has, we ought to spend our time trying to understand what *motivates* these other people. You've got to get this information from every conceivable source" (Harriman interview).

6. *Think of alternate solutions on these bases.*

Ideas should include solutions favored by the other side, solutions of one's own, and new solutions that combine the two in various ways. They should involve attempts to build on the earlier definitions and referents.

7. *While such studies are going on at home and contacts are being made to persuade the other party about the negotiability of the problem, talks can also begin in order to hear the other party's point of view.*

Much of his message may well come from a broken record, repeating the positions that have been publicly expressed many times before and reaffirming the pledges he has made to his own audience back home. But some of the message may be different. Often the need to explain one's position to others puts new strains on its coherence and credibility which allow ideas for new outcomes to appear. Although it is still too early to begin proposing solutions, it is worthwhile listening to the other party's declarations and explanations, in order to supplement the studies being made, and to make one's own case before the other party in order to help him get his own study straight.

In the preceding, it is as important to answer the same questions about the other party's perception of things—at the same time as that party develops a better understanding of its own position—as it is to clarify one's own standpoint. Understanding how the other party thinks is a good way to avoid surprises, and a useful way too of preparing to help the other party rearrange his perceptions to arrive at positions more easily compatible with one's own. At the end of the first round of SALT meetings with the Russians, the American negotiators said, "We were so absorbed in our definitional problems, we made no serious effort to anticipate theirs" (Newhouse 1973, p. 176).

Understanding what makes the other side run is not the same thing as sharing its pace; while there is no point in merely opposing the other party's goals simply because they are his, one does not have to espouse these goals in order to understand them either. It is important to include those items that one party does not wish the other to attain—the *interdiction goals*—as well as the items one wants to obtain for oneself—the *possession* goals. Some situations involve only conflicts in claims, in which what each party achieves is more important to it than what the other achieves, whereas there are other situations where it is more important to deny certain achievements to the other party than to attain them oneself.

There is a beguiling simplicity to the position taken by many governments that the only interests that should be taken into account in the prenegotiation period or even during the actual negotiations are their own, and that by force, deviousness, or any other technique one pursues one's objectives. J. Robert Schaetzel, a U.S. negotiator who has extensive experience in trade and disarmament matters, sees this notion resting on the assumption that:

> the other side is doing the same thing, so you are going to have a collision of forces, and out of this battle something is going to emerge, and that something is a result of the conflict. Obviously this is infinitely easier than negotiation, because the mere word is that you are trying to have some kind of amicable resolution of an issue. . . . I would submit there is a plausibility to the other course. It requires no imagination, it really doesn't require any skill, and it's particularly easy for a country as strong as the U.S. (Schaetzel interview)

But this method is inappropriate for the orderly resolution of conflict in any other world but one in which Darwin's rule of survival of the strongest might apply.

4

Defining Solutions: The Formula Phase

Phases, like ages, are organizing concepts that help us understand reality; unlike gears, for example, they are not part of the reality itself. As we have seen, in the negotiating process a lot has taken place between the beginning of the first phase and the second. The parties have decided to explore the possibility of negotiating, have made their own studies and prepared themselves for discussions, and have begun exploratory talks either directly or through third parties to sound out the other's intentions and to float their own ideas.

The exploratory and diagnostic process may go on over an extended period of time, with parties bobbing, ducking, and weaving, sometimes coming close to a commitment to resolve disagreements and then perhaps backing off from it. At some stage, an important Turning Point of Seriousness has been reached: the perception by each side that the other is serious about finding a negotiated solution—that is, that the other is willing to "lose" a little to "win" a little rather than win or lose all in a non-negotiated approach. If the other side is not perceived as willing to give *and* take or concede *and* receive, then it is unlikely the second phase will begin. Even when it does, the diagnostic activities do not end. They continue into the next two phases, for the parties must continually plumb and verify their own and the other's positions since the negotiation process itself continually brings new implications to light and by its nature changes parties' positions.

This turning point need not occur simultaneously for both sides, and it does not necessarily correspond to any formal moment in the train of events, such as the beginning or end of a conference. Depending on the degree of familiarity existing between the parties, the turning point may be achieved through an exchange of communications preceding a conference, through the process of arriving at a formula, or through an actual agreement resolving minor issues in the whole problem area, or anywhere in between. When the talks began in Helsinki in November 1969, the Soviet commitment to SALT was tentative, but after one month of preliminary talks it became clear that the Soviet leadership had given its firm approval to the SALT process, having judged that the United States was indeed interested in serious negotiations.

In prolonged negotiations, the Turning Point of Seriousness may even have to be renewed several times. One or more of the parties may go the negotiating table with no intention or desire to reach a negotiated settlement, as we have seen, but find it beneficial for other reasons to give the appearance of participating in a negotiation. In fact, it should be clearly understood that the road from the start of the second phase until agreement on the formula is registered may be long, convoluted, and time-consuming. In the process, each party may several times doubt the resolve of the other side to reach agreement.

Secretary Kissinger went to Panama City in February 1974 to initial a set of eight principles that were to serve as guidelines for working out the new treaty. To the Study Mission sent to Panama in November 1975 by the House Committee on International Relations, this action marked the turning point in the negotiations for the Panamanians: "The signing of the eight principles had a significant and positive impact on Panama's confidence in this new effort to draft a mutually acceptable treaty. Many Panamanians felt for the first time that they could negotiate on grounds where they knew they would get something new. After the delineation of these principles it was relatively easy for the parties to identify the major issues that would be the subject of detailed negotiations." Three years later, after the longest session of those detailed negotiations had been completed under Kissinger's successor, the Turning Point of Seriousness was renewed in strength. During the session a Panamanian delegate exclaimed: "For the first time we know you mean business," and an American official remarked: "Almost for the first time we got the sense that they understood our political problems. They now indicate an awareness of what we need in the United States to get a treaty and get it carried out" (*New York Times*, May 29, 1977).

WAYS OF REACHING AGREEMENT

Once parties are convinced that a mutually acceptable resolution of their disagreements is possible, they have two basic ways of arriving at an agreement. One is inductive—to put the agreement together piecemeal, building it primarily through mutual compromise or exchanged concessions on specific items. The other is deductive—to establish first the general principles, or formula, governing the issues susceptible of solution and then work out the implementing details. In the first case, detailed points of agreement are arrived at discretely, without specific attention to the broader implications or the relations among these points of agreement. In the second, the detailed points of agreement are suggested by the overall framework. Although the two approaches may appear diametrically different they frequently are in fact related. (See Levi 1949, pp. 8–9, for similarities in the process of legal reasoning.)

To draw a parallel, even an argument developed extemporaneously as a succession of debating points can be shown after the fact to have emphasized certain issues, values, and concerns, and to have displayed a certain underlying structure, even if there may be discontinuities and contradictions among the points. An argument that starts from an enumeration of a body of principles and then proceeds to their application to the case at hand also has its structure and specifics, and it probably shows greater coherence and cohesion than the extemporaneous case. Although it is doubtful whether the parties always consciously choose between a deductive and inductive approach, it is our thesis that they should be aware of the choices in approach to a negotiation and choose wisely.

There are occasions when the deductive approach may simply not be possible: If the two parties have irreconcilably different perceptions or conceptions of the problem and are unable to harmonize them, they may nevertheless be able to agree on certain details even though they attach different meanings to them; pushing a deductive approach in this case could prevent agreement. Such views may stem from culture or ideology, or may reflect the force and outcome of domestic pressures exerted on national legislatures. These forces complicate negotiation by inhibiting construction of a formula, but they do exist and must be taken into account.

The negotiations between Begin's Israel and Sadat's Egypt in the late 1970s will probably go down in history as the classic case of conflict between inductive and deductive approaches, quite apart from the differences of substance separating the two parties. Soon after the actual negotiations began in January 1978, President Sadat abruptly withdrew his delegation from the meetings in Jerusalem. The Egyptians had been pressing publicly for Israeli acceptance of a shared set of principles on which a comprehensive settlement should be based. The two chief principles stressed were (1) Israeli withdrawal from all territories captured after the 1967 war in exchange for a peace treaty and (2) self-determination for the Palestinian people. The first was simply an expression of the basic Security Council Resolution 242 formula: "security for territory." The Israelis, on the other hand, went into the negotiations prepared to bargain and trade concessions on each separate element in the dispute. They viewed Egyptian attempts to secure agreement on principles as an effort to impose preconditions for the negotiations. As a result of the clash between the two different procedural approaches, negotiations broke down.

However, another view might be that whatever the procedural differences, the Israeli view contained an entirely different formula or interpretation of the situation, which might better be bypassed in a search for detailed agreements since the two formulas could not be reconciled. The parties to the conflict defined the situation differently—the Arabs viewed Israeli occupation of former Arab territory as expansion, while in the prenegotiation period many Israelis argued that the occupation was something else. "Defensible borders are vital to Israel not out of any desire to annex territories, per se, not out of a desire for territorial expansion, and not out of any historical and ideological motivation. Israel can compromise on territory but it cannot afford to do so on security. The entire rationale of defensible borders is strategic," in the view of former Israeli Foreign Minister Yigal Allon (1976, pp. 49–50). Whether the annexed territories were defined as willfully expansionist or necessary strategic possessions could, of course, greatly affect the outcome of the negotiations.

Faced with this difficulty in finding a perceptual base from which to work deductively toward agreement, Sadat tried to maintain the approach but restructure the perception. Six months before his dramatic gesture in Jerusalem, Sadat tried to show how the situation, which was generally frozen if seen as a territorial problem, was flexible if security was the "name of the game."

> No Arab leader could cede even a centimeter of territory to Israel, even if he wanted to. It is simply impossible, especially in Sinai and the Golan. As for West Jordan, where the frontier was not definitively established, minor rectifications could be negotiated, for example to unite villages which were divided by the armistice line. . . . It is ridiculous to suppose that a few kilometers of land are indispensable to the security of Israel. We have surface-to-surface missiles that can reach Israeli cities from the west bank of the Suez Canal. On the other hand, we are prepared to discuss an entirely different arrangement, including the creation of demilitarized zones on both sides of the border, capable of guaranteeing the security of all the belligerents. (*Le Monde*, April 4, 1977).

These differences are also illustrated by the problem of negotiating the very complicated issues that concern international non-tariff barriers. The International Chamber of Commerce proposed that countries subscribing to GATT should adopt a "Declaration of Intent," which would bind governments not to introduce any new non-tariff obstacles or make more restrictive those already in force. Yet in the view of a former White House trade negotiator, negotiating such a broad declaration was inherently impossible. "Most governments find themselves compelled by domestic considerations to continue to alter old laws and regulations and introduce new ones, many of which can have trade effects. These normal and legitimate changes could not readily be stopped by an international agreement, nor should they be" (Malmgren 1972, pp. 206–07).

Without a broad declaration on how to proceed, the approach members have adopted in practice is to enumerate trade problems in a piecemeal fashion. But this approach without policy design has tended to prevent the development of specific solutions. "Countries cannot even agree on the general choice between a negotiating process which allows solution of one problem at a time and a process which requires a comprehensive global package of solutions which must be simultaneously arrived at. . . . The present manner will lead to a few results, a great deal of boredom in governments, and much frustration for industry and agricultural interests" (Ibid.).

But usually the deductive approach based on a formula for agreement is both present and desirable in successful negotiations. It is desirable, first, because a formula or framework of principles helps give structure and coherence to an agreement on details, helps facilitate the search for solutions on component items, and helps create a positive, creative image of negotiation rather than an image of concession and compromise. As one U.N. ambassador phrased it, "One needs some stable criteria or conditions with which you will be dealing before formulating negotiating positions" (Jackson interview). Ernst van der Beugel, who represented the Netherlands at the European Community deliberations, recalled how crucial a framework of principles had been in the creation of the Common Market: "In the negotiating process [Paul-Henri] Spaak took the line that you had to agree on twelve or fourteen basic points before starting the negotiations. If he would not have tackled it in that way I don't think you would have a Common Market today. . . . They negotiated two years on the details. But [Spaak] could say at a certain moment, "That's what we already agreed upon in the beginning" (Van der Beugel interview). At the May 1978 OPEC meeting, when price rises were in the air, Iranian Oil Minister Mohammed Yeganeh explained,

"We don't want to do anything to disturb the world economy. We are in agreement to produce all the oil the world needs but must not produce so much as to make a glut in the market. . . . So now the question is how to narrow the gap before Geneva," to which the Indonesian Deputy Oil Minister added, "It [the gap] is not yet quantified. No one's talking about figures" (*New York Times*, May 6–7, 1978). The two were discussing the need for a formula before fixing details.

Thus, the deductive approach to negotiations is more widely present than may be imagined at first glance. Often it is the conscious strategy of the parties, as a way to create agreement. But there are other relations between formula and detail than simply having the first lead to the second. For example, when unable to work out a formula directly, parties may try to turn the process around and arrive at a formula after initial agreement on some of the details; indeed, phase one, with its search for information and a few trial agreements on minor matters, can be interpreted in this sense. In other cases the framework of principles is implicit (as in many wage negotiations where the issue at stake is "merely" one big detail within a generally accepted context of principles) or even explicit but outside the negotiating process (as in association agreements with the European Economic Community (EEC), where "association" itself defines the specific items to be decided).

Both approaches will be covered in this chapter and the next, but, since situations differ, only parts of this discussion sion may be applicable to any given situation. This chapter will deal with those situations—the majority of cases— where the search for a formula constitutes the main substance of the negotiation, whether that formula is to be invented or discovered. The next chapter will discuss the phase that follows the establishment of the formula, or the procedure to be used if a formula is not appropriate. But to do all this, one must first understand what a formula is.

RECOGNIZING A FORMULA

The notion of formula is somewhat harder to identify than concession and compromise, if only because it rejects the idea of fixed positions and discrete moves. Formula is best characterized as a shared perception or definition of the conflict that establishes terms of trade, the cognitive structure of referents for a solution, or an applicable criterion of justice. These three characterizations are different but related facets of the same concept, but they will be discussed separately to make that concept as clear as possible.

A Shared Perception

All perceptions are selective. No one perceives everything that there is about a situation or a relationship. Even those elements that each side may describe as "facts" can be perceived in quite different ways; the salience or meaning of the facts may be different to different parties, a problem particularly pronounced in dealings between parties of different cultures. For the most part, perception is determined by the needs, goals, and experiences of a party. The parties try to communicate their perceptions on these bases, but often they assume what needs to be expressed and the meaning of the facts they see never gets through to the other side. As U.N. ambassador Rashleigh Jackson counseled, "If you can get people to state their principles, it helps to determine the kinds of axioms they are bringing to the negotiation. Then one moves to the modalities of working out principles."

In the preliminaries of phase one, the prenegotiation or diagnostic phase, each party tries to make these meanings plain and to understand how the other party perceives or defines the conflict. ("Conflict" itself is a matter of definition; defined in another way it could be called "competition"!) At the same time each party does its best to ensure that its definition of the situation is the one to govern the interaction. When they look for a formula, in phase two, the parties try to find a definition of the situation that will meet the requirements of both sides and at the same time will permit a solution. This formula can be quite complicated, or it can be a basically simple concept which allows other more complicated elements of the problem to fall into line.

A good example of a simple concept for bringing two conflicting perceptions of an issue into focus is the "neutralization formula." In many cases two parties see the outcome of a situation as a zero-sum: for example, when each party wants to possess the whole of a given territory lying between them, attainment of either party's goal would result in denial of the other's. Even partial attainment by partition is not considered acceptable for various reasons, including the unity of the territory and the refusal of either party to allow the other to hold any of the territory at all. But as soon as the parties realize that these two conditions—the unity of the territory and its denial to the other—are their real concern, rather than their possession of the territory itself, it then becomes possible for them to agree on a neutralization formula by which the whole territory will be denied to both, a solution that is accessible and acceptable to both parties at the same time. Upon agreement to this formula, negotiators can then turn to the implementing details of the solution, notably the ways by which this mutual denial can be rendered sure and credible. This was the process that underlay negotiations on Quneitra and the Mitla and Giddi passes in 1974–75, on Laos (1960–61), on Austria (1953–55), and the unsuccessful European proposal on Afghanistan in 1980. Even though the actual details of application were in each case different, as the situation required, the formula that permitted agreement was conceptually the same.

Much of the discussion in SALT I was an effort to find a formula covering the acceptable portions of strategic arms limitation on which agreement could be reached. Already in phase one of the negotiations in the fall of 1968, before the Turning Point of Seriousness had been achieved, the White House task force prepared nine "options," labeled one to seven plus two variations. The beginnings of a formula were established in secret exchanges between Washington and Moscow on the common principles of mutual deterrence, military parity, and strategic stability. After Russian views had been heard in the first SALT round, the American options were reduced to four (labeled A to D) in the winter of 1970. These established terms of trade between limitations on anti-ballistic missiles (ABM) and multiple independently targeted reentry vehicles (MIRV) on one hand, and ballistic missiles (offensive weapons) on the other; to these was added a fifth option (E) in the middle of 1970, after the second round. Option E shifted the terms of trade from MIRVs to ABMs and offensive weapons, providing the basis of the formula for terms of trade in the fourth round, in the "parameters of May 20," 1971, a year before the final agreement. This formula was then spelled out further in the fifth round in September, by various proposals termed "3 or 1," "2 or 1," "1 for 1," "zero," or "1 plus 1," referring to various combinations of ABM and intercontinental ballistic missile (ICBM) sites to be embodied in the final agreement. "As intended, the May 20 agreement did break the stalemate by removing the snags: the nonnegotiable elements of both positions" (Newhouse 1973, p. 218; cf. pp. 176–248; Garthoff, 1977, p. 8).

Another terms-of-trade formula which established a common perception of a solution was devised in the 1967 Assembly of the Organization for African Unity (OAU) between a Nigeria that refused any OAU interference in the Biafran war and a group of other African heads of state who demanded an OAU role. To reconcile these two diametrically opposed views, the late President William Tubman of Liberia proposed a "consultative committee" sent "to the

Head of the Federal Government of Nigeria to assure him of the Assembly's desire for the territorial integrity, unity and peace of Nigeria," as the final resolution read. The Nigerian head of state, "General Gowon, somewhat reluctantly, consented to the OAU formula" (Stremlau 1977, p. 93). The tradeoff was one of form for substance, in which both sides got something but less than they demanded. The tradeoff was not just an exchange of "apples for oranges" but rather a single coherent perception that contained both elements.

A final example comes from the Law of the Sea negotiation: the United States in 1976 sought to reconcile the competing demands for deep sea mining by an international enterprise versus mining by individual states and private companies by proposing a "double access formula" under which it would be possible for both operations to function. When this proved unacceptable, the United States in 1977 put forward the "banking formula," whereby an individual state or company would propose two sites, one for the international enterprise and one for itself.

In all these cases, the proposed or agreed solution to the conflict was framed by a relatively simple definition or conception of an outcome. It is not the word "formula" that is significant, but whether the proposal does in fact encompass the essence of both parties' demands and prove useful in guiding negotiators to work out detailed ways of meeting them.

Joint Referents

Referents are the secondary or underlying values that give meaning to the items under discussion. A bargainer who has been making incremental improvements on his offering price for an item may suddenly dig in his heels, not because of a special strategy or a calculation of concession rates but because the last item is all he has in his pocket; similarly, a bargainer acting the same way in a discussion about a raise may need the specific sum he is insisting on to buy a refrigerator or make a new tax bracket worthwhile. Money on hand, refrigerator prices, and tax brackets are the referents of these negotiations, and if they—instead of just the monetary value that triggers heel-digging—are known, a bargain can be struck where none was possible before. The other party can then respond, "Give me $X+2$ and you can pay me the difference of $2 tomorrow," "I can only pay you $X-2$ but I know where you can get just as good a refrigerator for that price," or "The new tax law leaves you worse off with X than with $X-2$."

In these cases the referents are simple; in most public negotiations they are more complex and need to be gathered together in a coherent structure. Many referents stand behind any isolated fact, even at the most detailed level, to give it meaning. It is the arrangement of a particular set of referents at the highest level that constitutes a cognitive structure for the agreement, providing the terms by which the situation is jointly defined and according to which the specifics for implementation are formed.

An examination of the Mideast disengagement negotiations shows the complex process of building a coherent package of referents; it also shows how one package leads to another on different levels of application, until finally the formula finds a problem that it does not fit and a new search begins. The process began in 1967 with Security Council Resolution 242 and its formula of "security for territory." During discussions of a cease-fire at the end of the 1974 war, Secretary Kissinger (possibly among others) suggested looking beyond a mere cease-fire to a different type of agreement and eventually developed a disengagement formula, based on 242 but more specific, which might be called "boundary-in-depth toward a settlement." The first Sinai withdrawal was based on the formula developed at the first round of Arab–Israeli talks after the October war (at kilometer 101), talks involving "thinned out" or limited-arms zones on both sides of a U.N. disengagement zone, in which the boundary-in-depth or series of three zones extended eastward from the canal. The alternative concept had been "a formula that would establish a cease-fire in place, with no further details, as in the cease-fire ending the 1967 war" (Golan 1976, pp. 73, 149). In the Syrian salient, the formula was the same—a cease-fire line in depth based on the 1967 truce line—and was imposed by the Egyptian precedent. The problem in the Golan Heights was that the withdrawal was not mutual, as along the canal, and therefore the application of the formula involved much harder bargaining between the two parties.

In the second Sinai agreement of September 1975, the new boundary-in-depth was justified, not by disengagement, which had been accomplished in the first agreement, but by movement toward settlement on or near the pre-1967 boundaries. There was basic agreement on the general area of the new boundary-in-depth but not on its specific location. The impasse over the two strategic Sinai passes was broken when the discussion turned from territorial possession to provision for the basic considerations of early warning and physical defense that the passes provided. It then became possible to put together a combination of U.N., U.S., Israeli, and Egyptian installations that would provide security while bringing about Israeli withdrawal from the territory without giving it to Egypt. Implementation was a complicated affair.

Kissinger . . . came up with an idea that would allow Israel to say that it had not completely abandoned the passes. . . . He would allow Israel to put its forward defense line at the bottom of the eastern slopes of the hills. Egypt would be allowed to bring its troops to the western slopes of the hills, and the U.N. buffer zone would be at the peaks of the hills proper. Then Egypt could claim it had forced Israel to retreat from the passes, and Israel could say that it had not evacuated completely. The other face-saver would be the presence of Americans in the hills near the passes. Peres . . . suggested that the Israelis keep the early warning device at Umm Hashiba in the U.N. buffer zone, but that in compensation the Egyptians also be given an early-warning device in the same zone. Then six more early-warning devices could be built and manned by American "technicians." The Americans would now have a constructive non-military function. Furthermore, they would be neutral, providing information to both sides.

The refined "security for territory" formula here was "neutralization plus balanced early warning equals security" and it replaced other intended formulas that the Israelis had advanced: "territory given up was to be demilitarized," and "the passes in exchange for an end to belligerency" (Golan 1976, pp. 246–47, 250). In each case, the previous formula served as referent for a more specific one to guide the new agreement.

When it came to the West Bank, however, "security for territory" in any of its forms did not cover the Palestinian question, and the momentum broke down. In the subsequent Camp David Agreements, the new West Bank formula was "security for self-government" (Article A.1[a]), which proved twice inadequate: first, by the end of 1979 when irreconcilably different interpretations of "self-government" became apparent, and then in early 1980, when it became clear that the Israeli notion of security precluded any self-government at all.

The formula as a referent basis for future actions is clearly discussed in regard to the 1977 negotiations between the United States and China on the establishment of diplomatic relations.

Vance with his lawyer's skills . . . can present them with
two possible formulas. They could openly say that they
will try to resolve the Taiwan problem peacefully, or they
could obliquely assure him that they will not repudiate a
unilateral United States declaration that, along with recognizing the Peking regime's sovereignty over China, ex-
presses America's interest in a negotiated settlement of the
Taiwan issue. As the scenario goes, either of these formulas or some variation of them would furnish Carter
with arguments to allay fears in Congress that he is deliv-
ering Taiwan to the Communists. And he could bolster
his case on Capitol Hill with an understanding from the
Chinese that they would tolerate the continued sale by
American manufacturers of weapons and spare parts to
Taiwan. As an inducement to Peking to play ball, the
Carter Administration is currently contemplating a further reduction of the size of the American garrison on the
island. And it may also downgrade United States representation there to the level of a chargé. (Karnow 1977)

An Idea of Justice

The coherent bundle of referents can concern many types
of values that give meaning to the problem and its solution,
but ultimately it can refer to an idea of *justice*. It may appear
to be overly good-natured and metaphysical to consider
negotiation as a process whereby philosopher-diplomats sit
down together and discuss different ideas of justice, but this
is implicitly what they are doing as surely as M. Jourdain
spoke prose. Although it is not necessarily helpful to a successful outcome to make that aspect of the discussion
explicit, it is useful for the parties to know what they are
doing.

For our purposes there are five types of justice. Therefore,
an agreement as to the type being discussed is already a step

forward. The first type—where all negotiations begin—is *substantive,* or partial, since each side chooses the particular criterion that supports its own side. Thus Israel talks of sovereign security as the criterion for a just solution whereas the PLO sees justice in terms of sovereign repatriation. If both sides were to agree to one of the principles of justice as the criterion for a negotiated solution and to its applicability to both parties, the formula would be established that could guide the search for a detailed agreement. Each party always believes that substantive justice is on its side, but sometimes the notion of substantive justice can be elevated to the point where it ceases to be one-sided, for example, principles that impartially govern a solution, wherever the detailed chips may fall. "Cuius regio eius religio" was the substantive formula for the Peace of Westphalia that satisfied the parties' idea of justice, and it was reproduced in the "leopard spots" or "cease-fire-in-place" formula governing the Vietnamese agreement of 1973.

The second type is *procedural* or impartial justice, the numerical justice of equality, split the difference, share and share alike. Although this idea may seem the easiest to apply, even to the point of obviating negotiations entirely, it is not that simple in a world where all items do not come in square boxes with a fracture line down the middle. How the difference should be split so as to preserve equal treatment is not always evident. Parties may also object to its application if they believe it totally ignores the merits of their case. In the Geneva Eighteen-Nation Disarmament Conference the West objected to the role the nonaligned participants were playing as they put forth suggestions which, the West commented, were "trying to split the difference at apparently equitable midpoints, irrespective of the justice or merit of the Western states' posture" (Ahmed 1967, pp. 38–39). In a strictly numerical sense, split-the-difference is most often used to dispose of troublesome details at the end of negotiations, but in a broader sense it was the basis of the boundary-in-depth component of the Mideast disengagement agreements.

The third type of justice is the opposite of the previous one in another direction, since it is the justice of inequality. It will be called *equitable,* however, referring to apportionment of shares on the basis of each party's particular characteristics. This is the justice of power, the right of might or of other endowments. In international relations, as in other arenas, sharing is not—and is not expected to be—on a numerically equal basis but on the basis of acquired inequality. More is expected by larger states, or more powerful states, or by littoral states, or by nuclear powers, or by victorious states, or by whichever party illustrates the axiom, "to those who have it shall be given." Equitable justice is a frequently used idea in negotiations (Messé 1971). The first use comes when parties decide to base their formula on equity; thereafter, they must decide which particular characteristic—size, power, coastline, atomic strength, and so forth—will provide the basis of equity in this case, and then how it shall be applied in detail.

The fourth type of justice is again the opposite of the previous one, for it is inequality based on need rather than power. If equity dictates that the strongest deserves the most, this type stipulates that the weakest deserves the most. It requires that to them who have not it shall be given, and is therefore termed *compensatory.* Under it, solutions are considered just only when they alleviate the unequal distribution of goods previously existing, and indeed it is frequently this very distribution that causes the problem that negotiation seeks to settle. Proposed formulas for agreement in negotiations on the New International Economic Order, and in association or membership agreements with the EEC all include some measure of compensatory justice. Like equity, compensation, once agreed upon as the basis of the formula, poses further questions about the particular elements of imbalance to be taken into account and then in what measure, leading the negotiations into their detailed phase.

The fifth type of justice is *subtractive* and it is the opposite of all others since it finds its rationale in removing possession from all parties. Since parties often want to deny a value to the other rather than possess it themselves, subtractive justice is frequently used as a compromise. The most common example is the null-possession or neutralization formula already mentioned.

The various acts and scenes of SALT provide many examples of the search for an applicable notion of justice. Beginning with a more recent episode, the 1977 attempts to revive strategic arms limitation negotiations involved an American proposal of several alternative formulas. Secretary Vance succinctly defended the proposal as possessing the elementary criteria for formulas: justice and comprehensiveness. "We believe that it is equitable and that it does attack the central questions which are involved in seeking a real arms-control agreement." But it was in the very terms of "inequity" that Brezhnev rejected the proposals. Fred Iklé, former director of the Arms Control and Disarmament Agency, summarized the contrast between the two alternative formulas in terms of justice. "To establish parity at lower levels, the side that has built up larger forces or is modernizing more agressively will have to give up more. . . . The only alternative way to reach equal limits would be for the side with smaller forces to build up more. . . . For the long run, if we are to reduce arms, we must maintain the principle that the side that has built up more has to give up more" (*New York Times*, May 11, 1977).

Weapons defined as strategic were previously covered in an equal-numbers agreement negotiated at Vladivostok in November 1974, replacing a lower but unequal-number agreement favoring the Soviet Union, which was part of

SALT I. In these earlier negotiations the winning formula—the "parameters of May 20"—was an agreement on equality in ABMs tied simultaneously to an agreement at less-than-equality in ICBMs.

> Moscow accepted the Kissinger preference for "equality" on ABMS, an as-yet-imprecise concept that would require a great deal of negotiation. . . . The Nixon White House . . . was conceding the Soviet Union a two-to-three edge on ICBMs—it was one thing to accept the principle of "equality" on ABMs, quite another thing to achieve it. One side was defending its capital city, while the other was planning to protect ICBMs at four different sites.

Newhouse's discussion (pp. 217–18) shows clearly the notion of formula—he calls it "principle"—as a matter of justice, determining who should get what, and the difficulties of implementing it in the stage of detailed negotiations.

The debate in SALT has been basically a matter of whether the principle of procedural justice (one-to-one equality), equity, or compensation should govern the formula of arms limitation, and which types of strategic arms should be covered (the question of the actual numbers under that principle or of actual arms—notably Backfire bomber and cruise missile—to be included under types is a matter of detail, not of formula, and is discussed in the next chapter under phase three). Examples can be given of other types of justice. The Panama Canal negotiations involved finding a formula of substantive justice, and specifically of finding whether the principle of sovereignty or that of defense would govern the joint decision on who gets what. The Paris Vietnam negotiations ended up substituting an agreeable formula based on procedural justice—cease-fire-in-place, who gets what to be determined by who has what—for an irreconcilably conflicting principle of substantive justice—

ousting the aggressor, who gets what to be determined by who deserves what.

The truce negotiation in the June 1967 war in the Middle East was based on the same apparently impartial formula, the cease-fire-in-place. The truce negotiation in the October war of 1973, as already seen, rejected the formula of procedural justice actually proposed by Foreign Minister Eban as being less than impartial in the circumstances, since the Arabs had made efforts to recover their occupied territory and cease-fire-in-place rewarded conquest. Therefore, the new formula was based on compensation, some territorial recovery for the party which had lost territory and had made an effort to regain it.

The Cyprus negotiations show a succession of complicated efforts to reconcile a number of principles of justice into a viable formula. Procedural justice is required but its basis is equivocal: equality of the communities must be recognized but equality of the individuals must also be guaranteed, tempering the community equality, since one community is four times the size of the other. Then, after the Cyprus crisis of 1974, equity enters in, since the power of Turkey has to be appropriately recognized. That recognition allowed for the cease-fire of July 30, 1974, and provided the pressure of the leading formula of "geographical federation" for permanent settlement thereafter. Unfortunately, for a solution at least, that formula leaned too much toward the notion of community equality for Archbishop Makarios and it failed to provide the basis for a final agreement.

A number of examples have been given of successful and proposed formulas in recent negotiations. Clearly, in each case, negotiation was not simply a matter of proposing agreeable but unrelated details; before the details came an attempt to nail down a principle or a notion of justice that could provide guidelines for the later determination of details and the allocation of benefits. The formula provided the referent criteria by which the question "Who should get what?" could be answered in detail. All of these formulas involved general considerations rather than precise measures, and therefore left room for maneuvering in the final determination of details. But they also supplied guidelines for recognizing when detailed bargaining on specifics went beyond simple whittling and instead implied a different notion of justice or allocation. Of this a striking example is the bargaining on "equality" in SALT I subsequent to the establishment of a formula based on the term; "3 or 1," "2 or 1," "1 for 1," "zero," and "1 plus 1" were proposed. Most of these were consistent with other notions of justice and different referents for details than "equality," and so were excluded.

> A case of sorts could be made for such disparity as 3 or 1: If the Russians were to have more ICBMs . . . , why shouldn't the United States have more ABMs to defend itself against them? . . . The case against three or one was more persuasive. For Moscow to agree . . . would surely have required Washington to endorse implicitly a permanent Soviet advantage in offensive missiles. . . . Kissinger . . . said repeatedly that zero ABMs was not consistent with the May 20 agreement. . . . The Americans, thanks to their patient exposition of missile defense, as distinct from area defense, had sold this concept to the Soviet military. Moscow's one-plus-one proposal was a sign of this. (Newhouse 1973, pp. 226, 229, 231)

One-plus-one was the final translation of "equality" and "missile defense" as notions of justice and referents for detail in the final formula.

An Egyptian analyst lamented the fact in late 1977 that President Carter failed to grasp the principle involved in Palestinian claims for self-determination: "What hurts," he said, "is that Carter and Brzezinski don't see that there is a principle involved, but seem to treat it like a labor–management dispute in the States—you give a little here, you take a little there and you come out with a nice package" (*New York Times*, December 31, 1977).

FINDING A FORMULA

Recognizing Its Characteristics

There is more to finding a formula than simply identifying a shared perception, a referent structure, or an idea of justice. The most important characteristics of a formula are *relevance* and *comprehensiveness*. The formula must naturally address itself to the dispute, and it must cover as many of the points of conflict as possible. Comprehensiveness does not mean that every part of the subject must be covered by the formula, but that parts related to the essential nature of major issues must be included under the agreement. If there is one major issue in the conflict, the formula must take care of it. Without attention to the heart of the controversy there can be no resolution. Finding the formula means confronting the basic elements of the controversy, and either dealing with all of them then or, recognizing their existence, putting some aside for later consideration. According to Arthur Goldberg, one should not enter negotiations with "an unwillingness to face up to what the real points of difference may be, in the fear of exacerbating those differences by pointing them out. It's the illusion that if you do not directly confront them, the difficulties will perhaps somehow be solved . . . without a direct confrontation of difficulties and problems. I believe this is very bad. A negotiator who is of that type will create misunderstandings, and very often bad consequences will flow." (Goldberg interview) If the formula is to be comprehensive and relevant, the major points of difference must be aired. But at the same time the "heart" must be defined in relation to the conflict at hand in manageable terms, and not in such broad terms as to be inherently unattainable.

The SALT agreement was possible because the parties were able to focus on ABMs and ICBMs, the heart of the issue, to leave out MIRVs, and to avoid seeing the conflict as only concerned with general and complete disarmament. In the kilometer 101 Arab–Israeli negotiations after the October war, Secretary Kissinger reminded Israeli Prime Minister Golda Meir that the global conflict had to be dealt with in manageable pieces when he said, "The question is whether you want justice, or you want the prisoners" (Golan 1976, p. 209). This is a point that many critics of Kissinger's step-by-step diplomacy miss when they charge that the disengagement agreements did not solve the Palestine problem: they were not intended to, they were only to lead to it, creating trust in smaller things until the larger question could be faced. Whether that was accomplished, or whether another approach could have done better, is a legitimate but a different question for debate.

Comprehensiveness was a problem in shaping a Mexican-American formula in 1980. The discovery of vast oil reserves in Mexico, the creation of complicated socio-economic problems by massive Mexican migration into the United States, and increased American worries over Mexican export dumping in U.S. markets resulted in renewed attention to Mexican-American relations throughout 1979. The two nations had different needs to be expressed in a web of agreements on a number of complicated issues of mutual concern—trade, migration, and oil. In the early stages of the Lopez-Portillo administration, some Mexicans called for an overall package of agreements with the United States on a range of issues. The United States, on the other hand, was unwilling to discuss an overall policy package, partly because of its desire to separate the oil question from other issues, and partly because of its desire to treat trade questions with Mexico only within the global context of GATT. "While the U.S. preference for global policies and 'delinking' do not satisfy Mexico's needs, and a 'package' is impossible for the United States as well as Mexico, a more integrated bargaining framework than presently exists seems plausible and desirable," commented one observer. "By this, I mean a bargaining framework that recognizes the complete range of issues at stake, and one in which the United States, precisely in order to advance its overall interests, would aggressively seek out new formulas for responding to Mexico's special needs, especially in the areas of migration and trade" (Stepan 1980, p. 668).

In the early 1960s the United States and the Soviet Union were trying to reach agreement on a comprehensive test ban, but stumbled on the issue of inspection of underground tests. Arthur Dean recalled American efforts to overcome Soviet objections to American insistence on inspection measures:

We had offered to let them fly their own planes; we had offered to have the windows darkened; we offered to have the people blindfolded; we offered to have Russian navigators in the plane so that we wouldn't be able to do any spying on the way to the site of the alleged explosion. I finally asked for permission to come home, and I said to President Kennedy that we had to divide these two treaties. "You don't need any inspection in outer space, in the atmosphere, or under the sea. Let's divide them, and you won't need any inspection. Then, we'll draft this thing and put them in two separate treaties." The treaties were separated in August 1962 on the basis of two formulas: a comprehensive test ban treaty with inspection, and a treaty covering space, atmospheric and underwater tests without inspection. The latter was signed a year later. (Dean interview)

The Simla agreement of July 1972, which resolved the issues of belligerency in the Indo–Pakistani war, was arrived at only when both sides agreed to omit the Kashmir question, even though it was the major outstanding issue between the two countries. It was not, however, the issue of the war that gave birth to Bangladesh.

As mediator in the Cyprus dispute of 1967, Cyrus Vance succeeded just because he avoided the global issue—the criterion for the allocation of power between the two communities—and instead focused on the relevant problem—the cease-fire—which had to be achieved before the larger issue could be handled. "It was not Vance's mission to get an agreement that would work [on the larger issue]—that, in view of the problems among the three countries, would have been impossible. His job was simply to get an agreement that would avert the immediate threat of war," a senior diplomat summarized (*New York Times*, December 7, 1967).

Principles which refer to only one or a few points can be subsumed under principles covering a broader range of problems in the dispute. Broad principles are not merely inherently satisfying because of their universality; they are more helpful because they provide guidelines for the solution of a larger number of details and they remove the dangers of incoherence and conflict among many smaller criteria. Arriving at broad principles is by no means a simple process, and becomes even more complicated when the subject under negotiation involves future technological changes that may have to be taken account of in an agreement, as in the various negotiations on disarmament (see Jacobson and Stein 1966, p. 501).

An extremely imaginative way of combining the parties' interests into an irreplaceable formula was concocted by Jean Monnet and his associates to deal with German remilitarization. After the Soviet attempt to blockade Berlin, it was plain to the allies that the absence of a German army weakened West European defenses. In September 1950 at the NATO meeting in New York, the United States made plain its position that unless there was an immediate decision to rearm Germany it might not take part in the integrated command. At the same time French opinion ran strongly against rearming Germany. The problem was to create German armed forces without creating a German army. In Monnet's proposal a way was found to combine the two positions: the creation of a European army in which national contingents would be integrated at the level of the smallest possible unit. Thus, while there would be no German army, German—and other—battalions would be distributed among brigades throughout Europe (Eden 1960, pp. 33–34). The formula was established at the broadest level, and combined two apparently irreconcilable positions. Accepted in negotiation, it was rejected four years later by the French legislature, even though France's Monnet was the proposer.

But the negotiating process is not just a matter of cooperation in finding a solution; the parties are still in conflict as they attempt to put across a solution that is favorable to them and their interests. It may be possible at times to devise a formula to serve as a framework for negotiations that is essentially neutral, in other words, that allows both parties to agree, yet not to sacrifice what each perceives as its main interests in the dispute.

Such is the case in the formula for negotiations on the Taiwan issue contained in the 1972 Shanghai Communiqué released at the end of President Nixon's visit to the People's Republic of China: "The United States acknowledges that all

Chinese on either side of the Taiwan Strait maintain there is but one China and that Taiwan is a part of China. The United States government does not challenge that position." The formula permits the beginning of negotiation leading to full diplomatic recognition. Yet until the issue of Taiwan was resolved with a formula on Taiwan itself, there could be no resolution of the conflict between the People's Republic and the United States.

At other times, one party may press for a solution that is still slightly more favorable to it than to the other party. The proposing party looks for a formula that will be favorable enough to the other side to attract its agreement, but still as favorable, or sometimes a bit more favorable, to itself. The slight difference between the two situations is important. When the two parties want different things or evaluate the same things differently, it then becomes possible to make up a package in such a way that each party gets (some of) the items it values most, probably giving up items it cares less about. There are other situations when the two parties want the same thing, or else one of the things they want is to deny the other party its favored items. In reality, the situation where one party does not care what the other party gets and the situation where it does are less discrete extremes than might appear in the abstract; negotiations usually involve both types in some measure. Thus, the matter of *balance*— the formula must be not so favorable to the proposer as to be rejected by the other side, but not so generous as to be suspect—is crucial to acceptance. Indeed, insuring a balance of interests in the formula is another way of indicating that it must be fair.

But if balance is not accepted by both sides each party is thrown back into a must-win mentality. This problem kept the International Commission for Iran from constituting the basis of an acceptable formula. For about a week's time in mid-February 1980 it appeared that the commission would succeed in providing the framework for resolving the main issues between the United States and Iran. For the Iranians, it would provide the opportunity to air publicly deeply felt grievances against the Shah, while for the United States it would provide the release of the hostages without the need for a humiliating apology for alleged misdoings. Ayatollah Khomeini threw a monkey wrench into the proceedings by announcing that the American hostages would not be released while the commission conducted its investigations. This announcement startled the United States, which had apparently agreed to the commission in the expectation that it would lead directly to the hostages' release. The element of balance was missing. Similarly, the Israelis saw it missing in some of the disengagement proposals they were offered. "First, the formula for the deal was asymmetric. One side of the equation was made up of substantive concessions and the second was composed of probabilities. Under the circumstances, such a deal could be seen as giving away something for nothing" (Aronson 1978, p. 287).

This sense of balance was captured well by Arthur Goldberg, who had been both judge and negotiator: "The best negotiator is not an advocate. The best negotiator is a man who could perform the role of mediator in the negotiations if he were called upon to perform that role. In other words, while he may have to engage in advocacy to reach a common ground, he should never be overly persuaded by his own advocacy. Advocacy should be a tactic and not an end in the negotiations" (Goldberg interview).

There is also a characteristic of human nature that makes it preferable to advance a flexible proposal rather than to offer a formula—no matter how good—on a take-it-or-leave-it basis. *Flexibility* is a term that can be interpreted so flexibly as to have no meaning at all, but here it refers very specifically to a formula's ability to be improved and amended slightly without losing any of its basic integrity and coherence. Thus, a formula that can be slightly improved by the other party, so that he has a hand in putting it together rather than simply accepting it, is better than a "perfect" formula presented intact and untouchable. The latter approach smacks too much of Boulwarism, the tactic of the General Electric executive who presented his detailed proposals to labor on a take-it-or-leave-it basis; labor negotiators were understandably riled, although the proposals were always made after careful study and were admittedly quite just and equitable (Northrup 1964).

Yet the mark of a good formula is not simply that it be improvable, but that it be coherent enough to maintain its integrity even after being slightly amended. Osama el-Baz, a member of the Egyptian delegation called back from Jerusalem in 1978, observed, "The Israelis don't realize that we didn't come with an artificially inflated bargaining position that could be whittled down." Contrast this view with the one offered in the *Jerusalem Post* blaming the Egyptians for the breakdown: "If the Egyptians entered not in order to 'haggle' but to secure traditional Arab demands, then Egypt has simply chosen the wrong entry. Negotiation that does not involve give and take does not deserve that name" (Henry Tanner, *New York Times*, January 20, 1978).

In 1957 in Geneva, the Western nations made a concession from their previous position that they would accept only a test ban that incorporated adequate control mechanisms as part of a broader agreement covering other areas as well. They now indicated a willingness to assign a new priority to a test cessation, which could become a part of a first stage of a disarmament agreement. After the Soviets announced their willingness to accept an international control system, the four Western nations agreed to explore the possibility of a temporary suspension while the control system was being established and also hinted that they might accept a loosening of the tie between the test ban issue and other issues. Because all of these proposals were tied together as one package formula, however, the scope of the concession was reduced (Jacobson and Stein 1966, p. 16)

The final characteristic of a good formula is its *irreplaceability*. Since the parties' aim after all is to have a framework that sticks, and since in addition the proposed formula must serve the interests of both parties to motivate them to conclude and observe the agreement, it is important to one and all parties that the formula not be replaced by another. A formula that obviously gives more to one than to another invites reversal. Irreplaceability is usually a matter of tactics and timing, but it may involve power and inducement as well: after couching and launching a proposal so that it sticks, one must buttress it and fend off attacks that might undo it.

In his instructions for handling the Trieste dispute between Yugoslavia and Italy, Llewellyn Thompson was directed to seek a framework for the negotiations that "would put Italo–Yugoslav relations on a permanently sound basis. We believe also that a package deal will enable both parties to accept sacrifices in a Trieste settlement that neither could accept if the deal were narrowly confined to the Trieste problem" (Campbell 1976, p. 171). The Trieste problem was to be put in the larger context of an overall rapprochement between Italy and Yugoslavia as a way to fend off attacks. Unlike the previous examples of Cyprus and Mideast disengagement, the focus of negotiation here was the global issue, and the larger context was used to anchor the specific conflict.

In sum, although there is no way of telling why and therefore when a proposed formula will be accepted by the other side, acceptability is in some part a function of its relevance, comprehensiveness, flexibility, coherence, balance, and irreplaceability, as well as of the skill with which it is proposed and defended.

Trying and Erring

Unfortunately, *trial and error is still the best way* of reaching agreement on an appropriate formula. A party may come up with a framework for agreement that is comprehensive, relevant, balanced, flexible, and seemingly irreplaceable, and still the other party turns it down. The only thing to do is try again. Since there is no innately or theoretically best formula for any problem, acceptability in the final analysis depends on the way the proposal is presented, the way it lands, the way it is perceived by the other side. Since it is still not clear in any conceptual way why one side accepts or rejects the other's proposal (as opposed to any of a number of alternatives), finding a formula is ultimately a matter of skill.

Making the first trial does depend on carefully answering the questions posed in phase one, the diagnostic phase, about the other party's position as well as one's own. The basic information comes from answering as clearly as possible such questions as "What do he/I really want and need for agreement?" and "Why do he/I want and need it?" As J. Robert Schaetzel expressed it: "A mushy approach in which the American negotiator is more interested in creating a friendly impression than in being accurate can be equally disastrous, . . . it is essential to create the maximum clarity in terms of what the issues and what the options are, and complete honesty, trying to develop an appreciation on each side of the limits that surround the ability of each side to try to arrive at an open compromise" (Schaetzel interview).

In 1969 Arthur Goldberg observed that one of the many problems with the Vietnam negotiations in Paris was a lack of precision in the way principles were presented:

> The North Vietnamese are urging the total withdrawal of American forces. The question is, are they urging this, or are they urging that we accept the *principle* of total withdrawal? There is a big difference. If they are saying "cut

and run, right away," that presents great problems. If they are saying, "We are asking that you accept the principle that American forces will not remain forever or indefinitely in the country," that's another question. (Goldberg interview)

The Geneva Conference on Indochina in mid-1954 explored the meaning and consequences of various territorial solutions to the military conflict in Vietnam, with most delegations focusing on a cease-fire in place. At the end of May the Vietminh changed position and proposed territorial jurisdictions under consolidated control, amounting to outright partition. The change appears to have come because Russia saw that the West refused a coalition-type settlement, and that therefore partition was the next best alternative for the Communist countries' needs that was likely to be accepted by the West. The new French government of Pierre Mendes-France also took up the same reasoning and the partition formula was adopted. When the French proposed the eighteenth parallel and the Vietminh the sixteenth, it was foreseeable that the partition would be along the seventeenth, and the other details also derived from the formula.

In preparation for the interim SALT agreement at Vladivostok in 1974, the United States proposed that parity should mean a Soviet advantage in total delivery vehicles to be offset by an American advantage in MIRVs. The Russians proposed a similar formula (with a smaller American MIRV edge) but wanted to include NATO and Chinese nuclear forces in the American figure. Washington then worked out a new formula of strict equality between the United States and U.S.S.R., with sublimits on Soviet land missiles (SSMs) and U.S. air missiles (ASMs), with its original formula of traded advantages as the alternative plan. In Vladivostok, Russia responded with a strict equality formula with higher figures than the Americans had proposed and a ban on American

ASMs, and the United States countered with a strict equality formula with a ban on all mobile SSMs, and then agreed to drop all such bans. "At this point, they knew they were going to reach a simple agreement based on equality of numbers" (Leslie Gelb, *New York Times*, December 3, 1974). A limit on giant Soviet SSMs was added, in exchange for higher totals than the Americans would have preferred, but the rest of the negotiations consisted of fitting definitions, categories, and figures within the formula.

While both sides are trying to make positions plain, the search for referents, criteria, perceptions, definitions, and principles already rooted in each party's stand goes on. Working on this level, it becomes much easier to find the elements needed to formulate a framework for the solution. Whether these elements should be opened up one by one between the parties, or simply pursued in a pack until they are all out in the open may well depend on the predilection of the negotiators or the peculiarities of the case; both procedures are possible. In the Trieste negotiations both sides made it plain that the agreements they were concluding on ethnic minorities and schools were all conditional upon resolution of the major territorial issue. Similarly, the element of verification has been a necessary component of any American formula on disarmament that implicitly links and dominates the other issues, while providing a context for the talks. "The Americans can neither propose nor accept anything that cannot be verified with reasonably high confidence" (Newhouse 1973, p. 14).

It is best to separate the process of gaining information from that of making proposals—phase one from phase two—as much as possible, lest the proposals be made before all the information is in. This said, however, even the process of proposing is a learning process; when a formula is rejected, the act and the reasons for it can help round out the information and lay the groundwork for a better formula.

The process of proposing, and the tactics of trial and error, can be improved by first preparing alternative formulas as well as simply gathering information. The alternative formulas should include possible offers that the other party might come up with, along with alternatives the proposer might find equally attractive, and then any other proposals that may be salient at the moment. The preparation of alternatives has several purposes: It reduces surprises, provides an array of "weapons," and whets arguments.

The nine options that the White House prepared even before the negotiations began in SALT I were viewed as building blocks:

> The idea was that the elements of each could be shuffled into various combinations and packages, giving great flexibility to the U.S. negotiating position. If the Russians frowned on some parts of a proposal when it was offered, the other parts could be speedily mixed into some alternative without dictating a renegotiation within the U.S. defense establishment of the entire U.S. position. All agencies would have already concurred in all the options. The building blocks, in short, would permit swift reaction to the Soviets, while minimizing bureaucratic conflict in Washington. (Newhouse 1973, p. 171)

A negotiator who becomes wedded to one formula has lost his ability to negotiate, since the formula itself becomes the non-negotiable demand. It just might be that the other side has a formula of its own that is better, even in terms of the interests of its opponent, an advantage that the inflexible negotiator cannot seize. But the greatest advantage of preparing alternative formulas is not in seizing the other party's acceptable proposals, but in being ready to counter his unacceptable ones and to shift to a new proposal if the first fails—that is what trial and error means. Of course, a serious and patient negotiator will not discard his proposed formula after a day's trial or come up with a new idea every working day. The search for a formula may go on over an extended period of time and perhaps over the course of several negotiations. Before a mutually acceptable formula is arrived at, it may be necessary for changes or movement in positions to take place back home.

One of the more puzzling concepts in regard to the preparation of alternatives is the notion of fallback position. Some alternative formulas may be rated *ex aequo* by their proposer and others considered less desirable but still acceptable. At the same time the party should have a clear idea—as noted in the previous chapter—of his security position, the value or acceptability of his position if there is no agreement. Somewhere in between there should be a minimum position, it would seem, an absolute fallback, and yet the very nature of negotiatory persuasion and argument is to make the other party reevaluate his fallback and minimum positions. Each party tries to persuade the other that the opponent can live and be happy with something different from—and eventually less than—what it wanted in the beginning. In SALT, in the Mideast disengagements, in Vietnam, in Korea, in Austria, in Trieste, and in nearly every case where an agreement was negotiated, both sides came out with less than a previously established minimum, and they did so by convincing themselves that, to get an agreement, a previously rejected outcome was not that bad after all. In brief, *a party should prepare its fallback position (even if it is not always revealed to the negotiating team), consider and reconsider its absolute minimum, and be fully aware of its security position.* It is the third rule that should be the least flexible.

The first reaction when one other party rejects a proposed formula is probably to stick to the original proposal, with arguments and inducements, for it is usually most unlikely for the opponent to simply agree at the first crack. Argu-

ments and inducements are discussed later in this chapter. However, if perseverance is not successful or appropriate, there are three other responses possible. *The negotiator can improve the proposal, or he can invent a new one, or he can exclude a troublesome issue.*

"Fiddling" may involve revising terms, or spelling out implications, or fuzzing references. Almost to a person negotiators urge clarity as a cardinal virtue, although much of the negotiation time is spent working out implications, consequences, definitions, and meanings of presumed formulas, until they are finally acceptable. At times, in order to reach agreement on a formula, "constructive ambiguity" and "functional equivalents"—two terms that gained currency during Kissinger's shuttle diplomacy—must be employed to draw up acceptable terms of trade. The latter means that the essential characteristics of the item under dispute become the focus rather than the item itself. "Constructive ambiguity" refers to agreement at some less specific level of principle or generality than the disputed item per se. But the disputed item must still be kept in sight, or the process of refinement may result in denaturing the formula, which must either be stoutly defended against disfiguring or be discarded. The earlier descriptions of SALT I, Vladivostok, Panama, and Law of the Sea negotiations all contained examples of successful fiddling with the formula. The Iranian Commission is an illustration of unsuccessful tampering. In the case of the 1974 Attica Prison riots in New York, functional equivalents were sought and could not be found. The parties and third parties failed "to find a formula that would for all practical purposes mean something close to amnesty without men like [Governor Nelson] Rockefeller and [Commissioner Russell] Oswald having to admit that it was amnesty . . . by the sort of ingenious formula lawyers are paid high fees to devise in other clashes of interest" (Wicker 1975, p. 69).

At some point, when the possibility of making small im-

provements in the proposal has been exhausted, new proposals must be made. Sometimes the new formula can be a rearrangement of the elements of the old one, a restructuring of its referents, or a reapplication of a criterion of justice. At other times, an entirely new direction covering new issues perceived in new ways is required. There is not special trick to identifying which of the two courses is called for; the negotiator must simply be aware that both are conceivable, then go back to his alternative formulas and see which is the better one with which to try again. The prolonged negotiations on the three Mideast withdrawals were concerned with intractable detail rather than formula; but both in the Paris talks on Vietnam and in SALT various attempts at reformulation and even change of formula were made until one finally fell into place.

Averell Harriman recalled that President Kennedy had been able to get agreement on a formula for ending the Cuban missile crisis by selecting the most constructive offer then on the table:

> President Kennedy got two messages from Khrushchev. He utterly disregarded the second, although some people were saying he ought to answer that with a violent protest. He took the first message, which was obviously dictated by Khrushchev himself. It was rather rambling, and he took a few sentences out of it, and on that basis he built an agreement. He tried to put himself in Mr. Khrushchev's shoes. So the general principle is, seize upon something that we want, something that is acceptable to us, and try to build from that point. (Harriman interview)

In 1951 there was still no peace treaty with the Japanese. In 1947 at the Commonwealth Ministers' meeting in Canberra there had been general agreement on the need for a tough treaty, but by 1951 only New Zealand supported Australia's

strong demand for a peace treaty that would prevent
Japanese rearmament. While refusing to sign a treaty that did
not limit Japanese arms, Australia was at the same time
pushing for a regional security arrangement of a permanent
character. The United States in 1951 wanted to conclude a
peace treaty with Japan, wanted Australia and New Zealand
to sign it, but did not want any provisions against Japanese
rearmament written into the treaty; its conception of a regional security system was one that would attract Japan to
the West. The formula conceived was two separate treaties
which would subsume the major interests of all three
nations—a Japanese Peace Treaty, which contained no provisions against rearmament, and a security treaty arrangement between Australia, New Zealand, and the United
States. The latter was concluded first, thus clearing away one
of the major obstacles to signing a Japanese Peace Treaty; in
the words of the Australian Foreign Minister, Sir Percy
Spender, "The problem of terms of the Japanese Peace
Treaty now became more manageable" (Spender 1969, p.
150).

The third possibility is of a different nature. Sometimes it
is not the structure of issues or referents that prevents acceptance, but rather one single issue that simply does not fit
into an otherwise acceptable formula. The parties can agree
to leave it out of their formula, even if it is a major question,
or they can set it aside for separate treatment under a different formula all its own. There are many instances where
mutual acceptance was made possible only by leaving a
major issue (but obviously not the only major issue) for later
agreement, or disagreement, provided that the excluded
item does not contradict the formula. In the Lancaster House
negotiations on Zimbabwe, the delicate issue of composing a
new national army was put aside, the parties agreeing to
work on this issue after the new independent government
was elected. In the Namibian mediation, South Africa ex-

tracted an interpretation from the Western Five stipulating that its troops would be withdrawn from Namibia but could remain if the new Namibian Government so desired, thus effectively postponing the issue. In the Camp David agreements the United States proposed that a temporary arrangement be worked out for administration of the West Bank and the Gaza strip, leaving the future of the Palestinian people to negotiation in coming years. Egypt and Israel were asked to agree on a set of principles to govern further detailed negotiations for an overall Arab–Israeli settlement, including the Palestinian issue.

SALT I provided major and minor examples of the importance of omitted issues to a final formula. The major issue dropped as unsolvable was MIRV. Until the MIRV–ABM linked ban was dropped and the formula was limited to an ABM offensive weapon limitation, the demands of the two parties could not be encompassed in a single negotiating guideline. That much was noticeable in the progression from the nine numbered options to the four lettered options described earlier. The path from option E to the "parameters of May 20" showed that other matters, such as the earlier Soviet insistence on American forward-based systems and the American insistence on removing the giant Soviet missile threat to Minuteman, had also been dropped along the way, in order to achieve agreement on what was agreeable. "Some of the significance of the May 20 accord lay in what it failed to say about some things and in what it failed to say clearly about others" (Newhouse 1973, p. 218).

Separating formula from detail was the key to the first Arab–Israeli agreement after the October 1973 war, on the cease-fire. "Mrs. Meir and the other ministers accepted Kissinger's explanation that it was the very lack of specificity that allowed the coming together of Egypt and Israel. Every attempt to discuss details at this stage might run the delicate agreement aground. It was preferable that the details be worked out after the signing, Kissinger argued" (Golan 1976, p. 114). Of course, disagreement on interpretation and detail arose immediately, but by then the formula had been consecrated and it led to agreement on details and held it in place.

A final example comes from a last minute attempt to bring about an acceptable formula, unsuccessful as it turned out but at least using the device of selectiveness among issues to try to shape a framework for agreement. Philippine and American negotiators spent almost nine months in 1976 bogged down over conditions for an agreement on American bases. One major stumbling block was the issue of jurisdiction over American personnel accused of violating Philippine laws, an issue charged with emotion and politics. In early December, Secretary Kissinger and Foreign Minister Carlos Romulo met at the Mexican presidential inauguration and worked out a new formula that would exchange one million dollars—$500,000 in economic aid and $500,000 in military aid—for a five-year agreement on base tenure. The supposed agreement was soon denounced by Philippine President Ferdinand Marcos, but not because it skirted the jurisdiction issue. The rejection was motivated by the amount and its division, and in the rejection the underlying notion of the formula itself was confirmed: a framework for agreement needed to establish a higher value for the bases, but need not include the previously intractable issue of jurisdiction.

Sweetening the Pot

Part of the process of finding a successful formula is making the other party accept it. At this point, inducements are first of all a matter of presentation. The means of persuasion already discussed—threats and warnings, promises and predictions—are generally incorporated in the proposal itself and must be used lightly. The proposer wants to make it clear that only good things will flow naturally from acceptance of the formula (predictions). Advancing threats and promises when the first formulas are presented is generally seen as applying too great pressure at an early stage, unless of course such side payments are part of the formula itself (as they were in the Kissinger Rhodesian aid plan, for example, or in the Lancaster House negotiations, where the promise of lifting economic sanctions facilitated agreement; or in the Trieste formula where inducements beyond the settling of the territorial question were an inseparable part of the deliberations).

Similarly, warnings that rejection of the formula will naturally leave both parties with an undesirable outcome can help shape the opponent's perception of alternatives, although if too heavy-handed they may instead stiffen resistance. After all, if one party tries too hard to show how unacceptable the alternative to agreement really is, the other may only be persuaded that it can exact a higher price for its agreement. The earlier-cited example of threats and warnings issued by the Americans in the Law of the Sea Conference evoked "don't-bully-me" responses, whereas the promise of greater aid was at least studied by the delegates. Kissinger was able to warn and bully in the Mideast disengagement talks precisely because he was a mediator and not a direct party; he also was able to promise and predict. This quick review of inducements here is intended to point out an important characteristic of the formula phase—that it tends to be a rather positive, optimistic, creative phase, more so than phase three, the search for details, to be covered in chapter 5.

Presentation also means seizing the initiative and posing the formula in such a way that it is difficult to refuse. Initiative does not always mean moving first, but, in the case of negotiations, it generally appears preferable to be the one to pose the formula—especially if one has discovered a good formula to pose. If not, valor doubtless lies in discretion, for the party who moves second has the chance to amend or tailor the proposal to his tastes. One of the American negotiators of the Non-Proliferation Treaty, offering advice that may be applicable only in retrospect, said, "You try not to have yours the last offer so the other person can counter" (Fisher interview). However, Secretary Kissinger is supposed to have said of the Vietnam negotiations, "The strategy was simple: Always be one proposal ahead of your rival and for each counterproposal reply with a new proposal. In this way you could always insure that your own proposal would be discussed." (Golan 1976, p. 176).

There are doubtless many ways of posing the proposal so that the chances of its being tailored in the direction of the other party's interests are minimized. The most prominent method is to couple the formula with an unacceptable alternative. This can be done in several ways. One is simply to present the chosen formula, on one hand, and to present the other proposals in such a way that their unacceptability shows. For example, the promises of satisfactory outcomes associated with the first can be contrasted with the warnings of unsatisfactory outcomes associated with the second. Kissinger used this tactic in selling the disengagement to Prime Minister Meir.

> In Kissinger's opinion, Sadat had two options: first, to try and achieve an agreement, through the aid of the United States, in a relaxed atmosphere. Second, to try and reach the same goal with the help of the British, the French, the Japanese and the Soviets, but in a climate of international crisis with the United States being dragged along behind the other states. . . . Several local incidents and a continuation of the oil embargo would be sufficient, Kissinger argued. Given the situation he just described, Kissinger recommended that Israel be generous. (Golan 1976, p. 153).

One can also use a member of his own delegation or, if there are several parties, another delegation in the same way, to play the "heavy" and remind the recalcitrant party that unacceptable alternatives are always around, if the preferred one is not accepted. Or else, if one represents a composite team or side, one can emphasize the difficulties of getting the proposed alternative together and warn that its rejection can lead to a much less satisfactory proposal that is waiting in the wings ready to spring. American delegations use Congress this way, and EEC negotiators can always remind their opponents of the difficulty in arriving at a common position and the danger that the next position might be very much less favorable. In each case the proposed formula is contrasted with a clearly unacceptable alternative. These tactics are tricks of presentation, to be sure, but they must not be transparent tricks. Form has a good deal to do with the acceptance (or nonacceptance) of substance, and the manner of presentation must be sincere and credible.

Striking the Iron

The same thing is true about timing. In a sense, timing is nothing: only substance and content matter, and if basic issues are not addressed directly the proposal will most likely be unacceptable. On the other hand, timing is everything, and there are a number of relevant theories of negotiation and of other processes based entirely on timing and the time factor.

At this stage, considerations of timing work only in the most general sense. The pressing, terminal effects of a deadline which will be noticed in phase three are not yet in operation, and the phenomena of bluffing, jumping, and holding out are not yet seen as typical. Yet there still must be a sense of time. The apt judgment of Cross—"If it does not matter when one agrees, it does not matter whether one agrees"—is applicable to an internal schedule as well as to overall deadlines. Negotiators in phase two are under the pressure of making good the Turning Point of Seriousness, which opens the phase, or, in other words, of showing that their judgment was correct when they decided that a formula providing the framework for serious negotiations was available. Parties often are heard to say in the middle of phase two, "They had better come up with a response to our proposal or a proposal of their own if we are to continue to believe that they are serious." Particularly if negotiations drag on after agreement has been reached on a framework, one party may come to doubt the seriousness of the other side. Private discussions went on for about a year before the conference on Antarctica opened, because it was felt that without some general understanding or a broad agreement on terms of settlement, it would be unwise to propose any formulas publicly (Taubenfeld 1961, p. 281).

In another negotiation the proposal of a formula at the right moment proved crucial. When Sir Percy Spender saw that John Foster Dulles was moving forward toward a security pact for the Pacific, he felt the time was ripe to bring the discussion down to the concrete: "Would it not be possible, in order to aid the deliberations, for our respective delegations to get together and put on paper the outlines of a possible draft security arrangement between our three countries?" he asked Dulles. No objection, Dulles replied, without commitment but with encouragement (Spender 1969, pp. 129–36).

If the parties can agree on a formula, it proves the seriousness of the negotiations and gives hope for and expectation of a successful conclusion. In phase two the pressure of time is behind the parties, rather than in front of them as it is in phase three. Yet, as in both earlier and later phases, the passage of time does mean changing conditions—a slowly moving target that must be captured by the formula. The right time in the negotiating rhythm and the right time in the evolution of the problem may not coincide, creating additional problems for the negotiator. A SALT negotiator discerned this problem in the arms talks.

> Another consequence of standing firm in 1970–71 [before the formula was adopted] was that when a freeze limitation was agreed, the Soviet force levels were higher in mid-1972 than they would have been in 1971. And the offensive freeze meant unequal numbers of strategic missiles. Again, I do not agree with those who criticize the Interior Agreement as being less advantageous to the U.S. than no agreement at all, but I do believe that it was less advantageous than a negotiated integral offensive-defensive agreement with equal numbers could have been. (Garthoff 1977, p. 14)

The Other Way Around

What happens when the opponent refuses to think formula? Some writers on negotiation have suggested that formula may be a peculiarly Western or even American way of approaching negotiations, and that other nations have their own ways. The problem of cultural relativity plagues any attempt to make generalizations about human behavior. Authors who have studied cross-cultural negotiations have often warned of the danger of assuming that an opposite number approaches the negotiations in the same way. In his essay in *Negotiating with the Russians*, Mosely (1951, p. 200) cautioned, "When stating a position it is well to be sparing in the use of general or broadly stated principles and when such principles are an essential part of the position it is necessary to remember that they are not shared by the Soviet negotiator." Arthur Dean, who negotiated much of the test ban treaty, has suggested that it is the Russians who want agreements in principle "of such vagueness that they will be able to interpret it in their own way and act to their own advantage while professing to observe the agreement" (pp. 45–46). However, the argument here is not in favor of a vague agreement nor, a fortiori, in favor of a conceptual statement that neglects its own application in detail.

The point of view adopted here is admittedly bold: we have suggested from the beginning that a search for a broad framework that will justify detailed agreements is both the way the best negotiators *do* proceed and the way negotiators in general *should* proceed. In this light, there are only two things to do if the other party refuses to negotiate first toward a framework of referents before settling the details.

On one hand, because of the advantages of the formula approach, the negotiator should persist on this track. There are many ways of doing so, as already indicated; formulas themselves can be built up from a discussion of specific points, and in fact do begin there during the preliminary period, while at a later time they may be quite explicitly the focus of discussion. The point is that in any case, to the analyst, negotiations pass through a formula phase: better they do it consciously and well than merely by accident. A certain amount of persistence and even a little effort to direct the discussions in this direction are therefore useful.

When it appears that the formula phase is being bypassed, closer examination may sometimes prove otherwise. In negotiations on the location of the withdrawal lines for Israeli forces in the Sinai, the first impression was of the parties inching toward an agreement by agreeing to small changes in the positioning of the lines. Instead of making successive changes in the location of the withdrawal line, however, the parties cast about for a formula for an agreement encompassing both a particular location for the line and the principles that justified its location. The standard writing about negotiation is often misleading. Referring to the period before the adoption of the SALT formula of May 20, Newhouse (1973, p. 218) wrote, "When two negotiating parties are far apart, they normally hold for some time to fixed positions, inching but slowly toward each other and the eventual agreement or failure to agree," when in fact the parties were not inching at all but probing about for a formula on which to land and big enough to hold them both. Kissinger, speaking about the second disengagement agreement, properly mixed his metaphors when he spoke of "talking about the same ballpark," and "inching toward an agreement," since at that point the searches for formula and for detail were going on simultaneously. The Panama negotiations are often presented as a matter of convergence on dates and durations, when what is really at stake is a difference between a formula based on sovereignty and one based on defense.

There is often a deliberate—although not necessarily total—separation between the responsibility for constructing broad frameworks and the responsibility for worrying about details, which can lead to some confusion. General Mohammed el-Gamasy, Egyptian President Sadat's subordinate in the kilometer 101 negotiations, was unhappy about the way the negotiations were going. "But, then, like Kissinger's subordinates, Sadat's subordinates were treated as mere technicians and entrusted only with details" (Sheehan 1976, p. 42).

On the other hand, attention to purely procedural matters may work against an agreement. If the other party insists on moving directly to agreement on details and considers a search for a framework to be a philosophical diversion, it may be best to humor him; the formula will come out in the process. In such a case, the first party should be working on its own formula at home, just to keep the issues and decisions straight and in proper relation to each other. Formula is not just an analyst's tool, unrelated to the work of the diplomats, so it is important to address the matter explicitly at some point, as an aid to settling details.

Finally it is worth recalling that many negotiations already have had the formula provided, in the negotiators' instructions, in the nature of the negotiation, or in a previous agreement. In these cases most of the negotiation takes place in phase three. Many of the points discussed here will still be relevant, however, for maintaining and testing the formula. Thus, the disengagement formula of a cease-fire-line-in-depth originally discussed at kilometer 101 was carried over into the three formal disengagement negotiations, where it was debated, tested, challenged, adapted, and applied. Similarly, the "parameters of May 20," which served as the basis for the SALT I agreement, were also the presumed formula for Vladivostok and SALT II, leaving in the former case only a second level of interpretation to nail down, and in the latter case a starting place for the next round of formula-making. Although it appeared that the result of the first round SALT agreements in May 1972 would be to stem the buildup in arms, it was soon readily apparent that competition and arms building increased rather than cooled. Based on the principle of equality, the agreement was severely criticized for the levels of arms it set, since with such high ceilings license was provided for each superpower to move ahead with all strategic programs. The failure of the negotiators to deal with technological innovations, moreover, limited its effect on force symmetries (Nacht 1975, pp. 106–08). Thus, SALT II began with a lot of very basic fencing over a new formula. On the domestic scene, wage negotiations frequently occur within an established formula, leaving the bargaining over details to the category of "inching" and "haggling." But in changing times when basic ingredients undergo serious modification, new formulas may have to be invented.

Caveat Negotiator

It is worth reemphasizing that phases are not neat, discrete time periods with long weekends to separate them, and the proper order of things may not be as achievable in reality as it is desirable in theory. Formulas worked out in the ways described here will generally produce the best results, but there are other ways of getting there. On some occasions it may be impossible to agree on a formula and, as a last resort, negotiators may try to pass from phase one to phase three and let the formula (phase two) work itself out in the process. There is little doubt that a diagnostic phase takes place, willy-nilly, and even if not done well, as is preferable, will be done implicitly; the same is true of phase two. Such negotiations stay on the level of details, passing from information to agreements without being able to establish a larger picture or a framework for the component decisions on details. This is possible; it is not the best way to proceed, and it is interesting to note that the parties often negotiate this way only after having tried to establish a formula and failed. In fact, they usually proceed this way in the hope that they will be able to establish their formula inductively, in the process of handling the component details, by extending the rationale for one point onto others, by establishing the stakes on which a framework can be constructed, or simply by creating a spirit that leads to a broader common perception of the problem.

Abraham is often referred to as the first successful negotiator. He interceded on behalf of Sodom, using an inductive approach to the negotiations (which may prove necessary when negotiating with some one so powerful). When the Lord was threatening to do away with the whole town of Sodom, Abraham asked, "Will You really sweep away good and bad together? Suppose there are fifty good folk in the town; will You really sweep away the place, and not forgive it for the sake of the fifty good folk in it? Far be it from You to act like that, to slay good and bad together, letting the good fare as the bad are!" To which the Lord responded that if Abraham could find fifty good folk he would spare the town.

The same reasoning was applied to forty, thirty, and finally ten good folk until it was clear that a formula stating that any number of good people arbitrarily being swept away with the bad would be cause to suspend the sweeping was accepted by the Lord, although never explicitly.

A more recent example comes from the negotiations leading to association agreements between the European Community and East African states. In the first rounds it gradually became apparent that the East Africans were not talking of association at all but of commercial agreement as a formula. The Europeans tried to get around the problem by shifting to details, hoping to build up to the association formula in this way, but the talks broke down because— literally—the two sides were not talking of the same thing. The talks were later resumed and resulted in the Arusha Agreement (Zartman 1971, pp. 97–115).

Since the obstacle to creating a formula in its proper sequence is frequently the inability of the parties to believe or perceive that a framework is possible, inductive construction is sometimes necessary to overcome disbelief. Secretary Kissinger hoped through a series of agreements on the Middle East to create trust and build a comprehensive settlement formula. When pressed by the Israelis on his views of ultimate borders, Kissinger responded: "I can't predict how it will all come out. What's important to the process itself is to keep negotiations going, to prevent them from freezing" (Sheehan 1976, pp. 43–44).

It is equally important to realize that a particular formula may prove inadequate when it comes to be implemented in detail. At that point the parties simply have to go back and start all over again, making a conscious effort to construct a formula.

The attempt to settle the 1956 Suez crisis at the United Nations was unsuccessful. Two points were debated at the meeting of October 13, 1956. The first part of the resolution,

which passed unanimously, laid down six principles on which any settlement of Suez should be based. The second part of the resolution, however—the operative part—although receiving nine affirmative votes, was vetoed by the Soviet Union. This killed the possibility of any U.N. action. In Eden's words: "We were left with six principles, and principles are aimless unless translated into action. The Soviet Union having vetoed part of the resolution which set out the action to be taken, no method was left for harnessing the principles. They just flapped in the air" (Eden 1960, pp. 562–63).

The American delegation in the Law of the Sea negotiations concluded that the "banking formula," providing two sites for every one exploited, might finally prove inadequate as a guide for agreement in detail, where positions still remained too far apart. In that case, reluctantly, the conference would have to go back to scratch and either devise a new formula or elevate one of the previous proposals to formula status. The head of the delegation viewed this eventuality with concern, since it would involve lost ground, lost time, and an opportunity for parties opposed to a treaty to strike out on their own with an independent fait accompli.

The Procedural Formula

As seen in many of the preceding examples, a report on negotiations frequently uses the word"formula" even where the present, specific sense is not implied. The word is also employed to designate a procedural device that allows parties to begin negotiations. The procedural formula is something more than simply the mechanical trick that might be implied by its most frequent manifestation—the shape of the diplomatic table. The shape of the table is important because of the substantive issues inhering in it, and the procedural formula is a way of getting around substantive obstacles and getting on with the business. Often it is literally a means of

bypassing obstructive implications, although at other times it foreshadows a substantive decision on some crucial issues. A recent case of the table's shape as a serious diplomatic issue came from the Paris negotiations on the Vietnamese war, where the configuration of the table was indicative of the relations among the sides around the table; as already discussed, the legitimacy of a party in negotiation is one of the major issues to be decided before negotiations start, and often prefigures the type of outcome that will finally emerge. The procedural formula in Paris finally admitted four parties—the United States, South Vietnam, North Vietnam, and the National Liberation Front (Vietcong)—grouped into two sides, thus overcoming objections from both sides to the participation of parties they regarded as not existing as independent entities.

Another example comes from the Mideast negotiations, which during 1977, before the Sadat initiative, had bogged down in a procedural dispute of great substantive implications over the form of Palestinian participation in the proposed Geneva Conference. A procedural formula was sought that would allow negotiations to begin: "We all have to distinguish between the start of negotiations, the bargaining, and the ultimate compromise," noted Israeli Foreign Minister Moshe Dayan. "I think ultimately an agreed formula will be found." Many were discussed, but the most promising one provided for an all-Arab delegation in which Palestinians would take part; after the plenary session, the delegation would break up into relevant national groups to negotiate the arrangements for the various borders of Israel. Israel continued to object to the presence of any known members of the Palestine Liberation Organization on the all-Arab delegation, to which the PLO replied that since all Palestinians were by definition "natural members" of the PLO, people without formal ties to the organization could still be acceptable to it. The procedural formula still was beyond reach

when President Sadat leaped over the issue and attempted to find a solution directly. But the Sadat initiative could not handle the substantive issue underlying the procedural formula, which was one reason why it collapsed.

Another procedural formula that took much effort was the arrangement by which disengagement talks were begun over the Golan Heights. The problem here was that each side held a trump card it would not play except to take the other's, and yet they were unrelated to each other, unlike the double encirclement in the predisengagement Sinai. The imbalance in the two sides' positions impelled Syria to bring in its only card, the Israeli prisoners of war, and make them part of the overall formula for the Golan talks.

> Kissinger focused on finding a formula through which Israel's initial conditions regarding the prisoners could be met while at the same time reassuring Syria on a disengagement agreement. . . . Syria would give Kissinger the list of prisoners; Kissinger would turn over the list to Israel and would receive for transmittal to Syria a proposal for a disengagement of forces on the Golan front; Syria would then allow Red Cross visits to the prisoners. (Golan 1976, p. 182)

This formula overcame the original zero-sum conflict between the two positions: no disengagement talks without the prisoners' list, no prisoners' list without a disengagement proposal.

Holding on to the Formula

The best way to hold a formula in place is to demonstrate that it works in specific instances by applying it to detail, showing its usefulness in providing guidelines for the resolution of component problems (phase three), as discussed in the next chapter. Once a formula is proposed, in fact, each side will study it for implications, applying it to details on a

trial basis to see what it means. This process is brought out into the open when the formula seems suitable to both sides and is agreed upon, and then is used to start solving the details. The proposer will also want to defend the formula by explaining its virtues and future usefulness. Such arguments involve persuasion and inducement, including predictions and warnings concerning the power of the formula and the consequences of discarding it, respectively, and also threats and promises. It is far more appropriate to use such inducements once initial agreement has been obtained from the other party, rather than before the formula is accepted, since in a sense the parties are being dissuaded from reneging or from acting against their own decision. Note the following example.

From the point of view of the Allied command in Korea, confidence in an armistice agreement could be present only if there were some means of supervision applying to both sides. It seemed unlikely that the Communist forces would agree to such an arrangement and, in Eden's words, "The Americans were no more anxious than we to contemplate the wrecking of the negotiations on such an issue, yet there was no denying its significance to the security of our forces." It was decided that, rather than hold up agreement on the armistice, the good intentions of the other side would be accepted up to a point and it would be announced that if they should violate the armistice retaliatory measures would be taken. The wording for this warning was "Should aggression be committed against Korea, the consequences would be so grave that it would in all probability not be possible to confine hostilities within the frontiers of Korea"; that is, China would be attacked (Eden 1960, p. 20).

The problem itself also contributes to the effectiveness of the persuasion. As time passes the problem or conflict is likely to get worse. However, it is likely to worsen unevenly, so that one party may see more advantage either in foot dragging or in an early solution than the other. Furthermore, the situation may worsen not by continuing, but by changing in character, again producing time pressures that are felt unequally among the parties. These changes need not actually take place; they can be anticipated, phrased as predictions or warnings, to press others into action. The situation can also be changed by a party's closing options, facilitating solutions, or simply building pressure of time, or again such changes can be threatened or promised before they actually take place. All of these changes in the nature or status of the problem can be used to hold or threaten an agreement on a formula.

The formula advanced by Kissinger in Rhodesia in 1976—economic guarantees for the whites, transitional political guarantees to the blacks—was rejected by Smith and rapidly bypassed by real and anticipated events in 1977. After the collapse of the Geneva talks, any attempt at revival, either by Britain alone or under joint Anglo-American auspices, was futile before it started. The new events had to be played out first and the success of such things as the Zimbabwe guerrillas, the third front of blacks who eventually worked with Smith, the Rhodesian army, and the new more liberal and more conservative white parties simply had to be tested. No matter that the general, not-too-distant outcome—Zimbabwean independence—was agreed to by most observers; the changing situation had to be allowed to run its course to a new stalemate before it would become clear how that outcome would be achieved.

Similarly, the 1972 spring offensive was a last attempt to verify conditions on the ground in Vietnam to see whether the proposed formula was appropriate. Kissinger is said to have noted later, "Hanoi played into Washington's hands when it opened an offensive that enabled the United States to renew the heavy bombing of the North and thus wear down Hanoi even more" (Golan 1976, p. 176).

BEHAVIOR IN THE FORMULA PHASE:
A SUMMARY

A formula provides a substantive framework for agreement and a set of criteria for resolving details. If it does not cover the whole problem area, as may often be the case, it presumably covers enough of it to make an agreement worthwhile. The search for formula is a time of intensive negotiations, usually a shorter period of time than the prenegotiation period (phase one) and one involving direct confrontations at formal sessions. During this period the tactics of the parties are focused mainly on finding a favorable and agreeable framework and making it stick, on one hand, and, secondly, on discarding other frameworks (of one's own or of others' invention) that are not favorable enough to merit agreement. During this period, too, the problem is most likely to be undergoing some changes of its own; the longer the negotiations go on, the more likely the changes will be. Whether produced by the problem itself or manipulated by the parties, the changes in the conflict provide arguments for one side or the other, supporting or undermining the formulas under discussion.

There are dangers at this point that may impede the progress toward solution on any terms. One is the danger that, for cultural or tactical reasons, the parties may be using different approaches to negotiation, and while one is seeking a broad formula the other is concentrating on precise details. Another is the danger that a formula is truly lacking, even among the best-willed students of the problem, or that the problem is composed of such conflicting elements that formulas would be contradictory and clearly inimical to the parties' interests. Unfortunately, since so much is a matter of will and perception, there is no way of telling if or when a problem is "objectively" impervious to a formulated solution. A third danger is that the search for formulas might impede the possibility of agreement on details, where the parties are much closer to each other, or might take precious time while the problem is rapidly deteriorating. In the latter two cases, admittedly, the parties are better advised to attack details directly, while keeping an eye out for helpful formulas. But such cases are rare, by the nature of things, and it is predictable that even working inductively the parties will find potential formulas—or else in a later stage of the problem they will wish they had.

If the search for a formula is pursued diligently, however, it will provide a helpful basis for proceeding to the next phase and creating specific agreements on details. Even if the process is lengthened by the discovery of contradictions and deeper conflicts, the formula will have been useful in bringing out the elements that require solutions. In the process each party should be referring to the following checklist:

1. *Keep a flexible and comprehensive mind-set, open to slightly or greatly different ways of encompassing the same things, or alternatively to including most items in the same package while isolating "the one that doesn't belong" for separate treatment or postponement.*

2. *Remember that the problem, not the opponent, is the "enemy" to be overcome.*

It is the problem that prevents good and beneficial relations and sours the other party's perception of things (including yourself), so the other party needs help to solve the problem, often against his own will and perception. Problems being what they are, however, this view of the other party is equally valid for oneself. Too often it is read to mean that one party has all right and truth and the other must be saved from its error. To the contrary, both parties are locked in the problem, often against their more considered judgment if they could disengage themselves from the grip of the problem and consider things "objectively." The negotiator looking for the formula must therefore not only evaluate his own demands and constraints but also put himself above these to evaluate the problem itself, in order to find a just and acceptable way of overcoming it.

3. *Do not be deterred by unfriendly behavior.*

Advice to diplomats often sounds as if they were emotionless computers, and yet even with the most dedicated application of strategy and tactics, the element of human responsiveness is often crucial. People get mad, or are flattered, or are tired, and the best intentions of following sound and scientific advice fall away. Probably the most enervating experience is to find a sincere (even if slightly partisan) effort of constructive goodwill met by deafness and hostility. Conflict is inherent in negotiation, and a certain amount of hostility is not only to be expected but is probably psychologically and certainly tactically necessary, lest the parties make too much of a common cause out of solutions and forget their own interests as defined back home.

How discouragingly often a negotiation turns out to be a dialogue of the deaf or, even worse, a typical cold war insulting match such as Panmunjon. At times like that, no matter how humanly difficult, it is necessary for at least one of the sides to remember that it has to think positively for both parties and help the opponent out of his difficulties. Without such awareness there will be no agreement, and presumably there can be an agreement, on some terms, which is more favorable to both sides than disagreement. There is no sure-fire prescription to cure diplomatic deafness and bad manners, and in fact sometimes a dose of the same medicine is the best remedy. The point here is merely that, discouraging as such a response may be, it should not deter the negotiator from pursuing his search for a framework for agreement positively and constructively—and even cleverly.

4. *Keep talking.*

Recesses, visits back home for instructions, and even a tactical stalk out of the room all have their place, but continued contact of some sort is of great importance. When contact is broken, reestablishment takes a special effort. New proposals can be floated through the public media, to be sure, but the process of exchange and exploration cannot be pursued without face-to-face communication. Furthermore, to a greater or lesser degree, the act of talking may inhibit other types of action, or at least require their justification. The agreement to accept Le's substitute when Le was diplomatically ill might not have prevented the 1972 spring offensive in Vietnam, but at least it would have weakened the public case for it, required a justification, and kept up pressure for agreement on a formula.

5. *Think of detailed applications while thinking of the broader formulas.*

Negotiators must juggle a lot of contradictions: they must pursue conflict cooperatively, they must think partially and impartially in the same formula, and they must work on the applied as well as the general level at the same time. Not all agreements go to the detailed stage; in some cases, merely a statement of general principles is required. But even in those cases the general principles must be relevant to something, and so, paradoxically, thinking formula requires thinking detail. It also prepares the negotiator—when required—to pass on to the next phase.

5

Working Out Agreements: The Detail Phase

Once the formula has been established, either by discovery or by invention, it can provide guidelines and referents for the solution of more precise problems, and the search for detailed agreements can begin. Again, it should be emphasized that the notion of two phases—the formula phase and the detail phase—is much sharper in the discussion here than it is in reality. There is considerable shading and overlap between the two.

Not only are the two phases blurred around the edges, there can also be movement back and forth from one to the other. Many analyses of the phases have been faulted for neglecting the possibility of backtracking. In negotiation, backtracking is a constant possibility; therefore negotiators must be aware that if they and their opponents cannot turn their formula into an agreement on details they must go back to reformulate a framework that works. The settlement of details is a formula's only test and can be accomplished only on a trial and error basis. There are times when speedy agreement on a formula is followed by a long and arduous search for agreement on details. Following two days of meetings of the Military Committee in Cairo in early January 1978, Israeli Defense Minister Ezer Weizman reported an

147

agreement on the principle of dividing the Sinai into three zones. But agreement on the details of the size of the zones was yet to be worked out, and Mr. Weizman described the road to peace as "long, very long" (*New York Times* January 8, 1978). In fact it took two more years. In this case as in many others the road from agreement on formula to agreement on details was bumpy and full of obstacles.

A final caution should be added on the use of "phases": The search for details itself may follow a process of criteria-and-application similar to the formula–detail process but at lower levels of generality. A theme running through this entire discussion is that the meaning and value of items under negotiation are not fixed in those items but are determined by an underlying or secondary structure of referents. This notion will be applied in the following analysis of criteria and rationale as guides to details, on down until the last small points are in place (or until a mechanism is established to resolve those left over or those that came up later). It is still useful, nevertheless, to draw a broad analytical distinction between the previously discussed formula phase and phase three, the search for agreement on details.

Most negotiations seek to settle a certain number of detailed points of conflict on which parties have a more or less precise idea of what they want. Formulation is difficult because of the innovation required, but detailing is difficult because of the hostility encountered. Dealing with details is often the most complex part of the process of negotiation and cannot be covered in a single model. A tourist out to buy a rug in Morocco has only two items to juggle—the rug and the price—and the bargaining proceeds in rather simple terms. The man who goes to purchase a used car engages in an only slightly more complex process (since, in addition to item and price, he juggles extras and accessories). The teams constructing a new treaty on the Panama Canal, on the other hand, have to establish details within the framework of a number of principles, trading off dissimilar items, converging from positions expressed in varying terms, not to speak of preparing a final document whose ratification depends on bodies physically and politically distinct, as well as distant, from either team. Guidelines for negotiating details (phase three) will have to come from a number of different, overlapping approaches or models, and include emotions.

SENDING SIGNALS

Bargaining for details has many functions besides simply finding a particular point of agreement, a characteristic that makes clear patterns of action particularly difficult to find. Negotiators respond to the other party's previous "move," but they also "respond" to their own previous move and they try to make signals to the other party (and if necessary to their own audience back home). Moves include "non-moves" as negotiators may attempt to convince the other side there is no more give in a particular position. "I couldn't possibly do what you are asking," "I would be exceeding my instructions to give you that," "Can't you see if you can do a little better?" are all moves. As a result negotiators *teach*, *learn*, and *communicate* as they make each move, while at the same time acting within the context of outside considerations—formulas, referents, contexts, principles—which give meaning to and govern the magnitude of their individual propositions.

In addition, this is all done in an atmosphere usually much more hostile than when the parties were looking for their formula. At the beginning of detail bargaining moves and non-moves may be exchanged in an air of cordiality, but as negotiations proceed tensions may rise and courtesies diminish. For in phase three the parties are no longer looking positively and constructively for a broad framework that will contain their dispute, as they were in phase two. Now they are trying to discover the detailed implications of the general formula, making sure that the other party implements his part of the formula honestly and does not upset the balance achieved in the formula. This explains why so many negotiations—the SALT rounds, the Panama treaty talks, the Paris negotiations on Vietnam, the Mideast peace process—have broken down in phase three after phase two had apparently been successfully concluded. The parties are continually on guard against the possibility that the other's acceptance of the formula is a trick, either to be withdrawn after concessions are exacted on details or to be turned to decisive advantage on some unsuspected implication. Too often there are critics back home who are only too willing to remind the domestic audience of this possibility. Furthermore, each party is continually on guard lest the other side circumvent the agreement on formula with a different set of details.

A striking attempt to destroy the formula with details took place in the Nonproliferation Treaty (NPT) negotiations, as related by Arthur Goldberg, the chief American negotiator:

> After we had a gentlemen's agreement with the Russians on non-proliferation—that no further amendments would be offered beyond those we had agreed upon—at the very last stage the Russians handed me a new proposal.
>
> I handled the problem very simply. I looked at the proposal, handed it back and said, "This is outside the scope of our agreement, Mr. Minister, and it's unacceptable."
>
> He said, "Are you saying to me that your government rejects it?"
>
> I said, "Yes." And I added, "I don't want to see it, I don't want to have it."

"Even for your records?"

I said, "Even for my records."

He said, "Don't you have to report it to Washington?"

I said, "No, I don't have to report it to Washington. I'm authorized to negotiate and I see no point in reporting it to Washington."

He said, "Does that mean that I can report to my government that on the highest levels your government has turned it down?"

I said, "Yes, you can report that."

He said, "But you haven't even called the Secretary of State or the President."

I said, "I don't have to."

He said, "And are you not going to report it, as a matter of interest?"

I said, "No, I'm not going to report it. I don't have it, Mr. Minister—I gave it back to you—I can't report it."

Now, of course, I did report to my government that this effort had been made. I knew what the reaction was; it was completely out of the ballpark. It was a ban-the-bomb proposal which they put in at the last minute, I think to satisfy the Rumanians that they were pushing it. They knew we would not accept it. (Goldberg interview)

In the SALT talks it was the Americans who tried to work against their own formula with a proposal for ABM sites that would leave a choice between 3 or 1. "The Soviet side immediately rejected this as essentially a replay of the unacceptable 4-to-1 proposal. And they saw this as a step back from the equal ABM limitation once agreed and clearly implied in the May 20 [formula] approach" (Garthoff 1977, p. 12). The problem was that the "parameters of May 20" do not appear to have been completely thought through by Washington, or at least all their implications were not evident—a common problem with formula agreements which must be struck while the iron is hot, leaving little time and room for lengthy study. "Later, it transpired that not only was the language of the May 20 agreement ambiguous, but that the record of exchanges leading up to it was also ambiguous and in some key respects (above all, on the question of including SLBM limitations) it was prejudicial to what the U.S. Government decided, *after* May 20, it wanted in the SALT I accords!" writes a participant (Garthoff 1977, p. 14).

Signals for Communicating

Parties continue to *communicate* information selectively about their own positions during phase three. Ever since the latter part of phase one the parties have been doing this but the work is not over. As negotiations focus more on precise points of conflict, each party has to continue to try to get across information about what it wants (including what it wants the other party not to have) and what it is willing to give up and why, but often without telling what it does not want or does not care that the other side gets. One side's bargaining chip may be the other side's bottom line objective. If only one of the parties had this information its bargaining position would be strengthened. If both parties had this information it would cancel out the advantage to one side. Since negotiation is basically a process of wearing down the other party's expectations and demands so that they can fit in an agreement with those of the first party (and vice versa!), each party wants to establish its demands in unshakable terms. But since vice versa is also true, each party wants to dissimulate its real aims, so that it may appear to give in reluctantly on things it ostensibly values in order to achieve things it really wants. There are limits to such bluffing, but it is only because honesty is the rule that bluffing can be the exception. If we did not expect negotiators to bargain in good faith, bluffing would not be possible.

Bluffing can refer to various types of communications: (1) reality of information ("We do have a nuclear capability," when we really do not quite); (2) hierarchy of values ("We prefer this island to that one but we will let you have this one if you give us enough compensation," when we really don't care about this one but can't live without that one); (3) degree of commitment ("We will bomb if you don't agree but will give aid if you do," when we have no intention either of bombing or of giving aid). Beyond this classification, however, there is little advice that can be given on bluffing since it is by definition an exception to whatever guidelines are established!

The trouble with bluffing and non-bluffing is that almost any information is inherently ambiguous. Bluffs are possible only because they may be real, bargaining chips have a way of becoming committed demands on their own, and rejected offers become acceptable offers when last session's minimum positions were unable to get off the ground. Since the substance of information is ambiguous, the procedural signals it gives off may lead to the wrong reactions. It may be advantageous to advance a "sham bargaining position," to probe for information on the minimum acceptable position of the other side, and this may also confuse the other side about the minimum position of the one doing the shamming. However, it might also lead the other side to believe that agreement is impossible and thus break off or, in any event, delay the conclusion of agreement. President Assad ran this risk in the 1974 Syrian disengagement talks, thereby gaining many small increments of territory until he gave in on the last demand (Golan 1976, p. 204). SALT led to the invention of the term "bargaining chips," but even Secretary Kissinger, its author, later rued the day he supported the cruise missile for this purpose, only to see it harden into a permanent acquisition when its military adherents would not let go of it (Garthoff 1978, p. 22).

Another type of communication, which has been used in labor negotiations to test the willingness of the other side to make further concessions, is to suggest calling in a mediator. The other side's acceptance may be taken as evidence that he is willing to explore further how the two positions can be brought together, thus indicating he has something further to give (Walton and McKersie 1965, p. 65). But the acceptance may also indicate a conviction in the rightness of his position and a firm faith in vindication at the hands of a truly impartial judge. In other words, the indication of willingness may give a signal of either negotiability or nonnegotiability. Such information does not cancel itself out because of its ambiguity and become useless; it is valuable, but it raises the need for additional information to clarify its meaning.

More important than such dissimulation is the accurate communication of information, values, and commitments that the parties give to each other. A common language soon grows up among negotiators, not because of any imposed culture but because of the implications of particular positions for the universal negotiating process. An unreasonably high opener means a play to the gallery rather than a serious negotiating position, since a trial midpoint in a field defined by the high opener would simply be outside the range of agreement of the other party. Giant step concessions mean that the original position was for show, and a tough stand can be maintained by the other party. These communications have both static and dynamic—or defensive and maneuvering—characteristics that convey information both about a position and about the type of movement that can be associated with that position. The two elements are, of course, contradictory, for the business of the negotiator is to defend and attain positions that are important to him, while at the same time giving in enough on the positions that are important to the other party to acquire his agreement to the positions important to the first. Since the demands of the two parties may concern different items but also are likely to concern some of the same items, the conflict in communications is evident. Usually a long time in the detail negotiations is spent making demands and their implications very clear, followed by a search for concessions that will make them compatible.

Vladimir Velebit, the Yugoslav negotiator on Trieste, followed his instructions to begin negotiations with a high opening presentation of Yugoslav demands:

> We had to fire off the so-called *baroud d'honneur*. That was rather repulsive for me to do, but I had instructions from my government to demand the whole Free Territory of Trieste. I had to put forward all the arguments . . . and I rattled them off, I think, the whole first week, keeping myself busy and keeping all the others busy. I was convinced that it was just a *baroud d'honneur* to show that we were trying to present our full case, and I am quite certain that Thompson and Harrison [the American and British negotiators, respectively] also understood it was a method for letting off steam. (Campbell 1976, pp. 94–95)

African negotiators preparing an association agreement with the European Communities in 1962 first signaled a position of principle ($1.8 billion in aid) and then dropped to a more modest demand ($1.135 billion) in the next bid. With such beginnings it is not surprising that the final figure was $800 million, actually less than some of the European openers which ranged from $1,275 to $681 million, although the paths to this final figure were not marked by neat steps, as will be shown below (Zartman 1971, pp. 44, 48).

Similarly, in the 1968–70 negotiations between the United States and Spain over base rights, an aid figure of about $150 million (compared with a U.S. opener of about $140 million) was not surprising in the light of the Spanish move from $1.2 billion to $745 million on their second bid (Tracy 1978, pp. 204–19). Those two moves signaled a concession rate that was correctly interpreted by the other side. On the other hand, when Prime Minister Dom Mintoff raised the annual rent for the British base on Malta from £5 million to £7.5 million to £19 million, he was signaling a very different, and essentially unpredictable, kind of negotiation (Wriggins 1976, pp. 221–31).

In negotiations between the United States and the European Economic Community over compensation for damages to U.S. trade interests by three new members of the community, the American trade negotiator, J. Robert Schaetzel, criticized the U.S. decision to open with an extreme position: "I think the fundamental error was made there by beginning with an extravagant American demand for damages which produced equally extravagant European counterdemands. Each side therefore got locked into mutually extreme positions from which they had a hell of a time extricating themselves" (Schaetzel interview).

Other signals come through the wording. As Garthoff (1977, p. 18) wrote of SALT, on a point banning "futuristic" antiballistic systems:

> For several months the Soviet side objected. . . . But eventually the Soviet delegation began to argue against the proposal as "unnecessary" and "premature" and "superfluous." These, as we learned, were formulations in effect signalling that while the Soviet side did not

want a position, they did not regard it as *unacceptable* if
we strongly persisted. Firmness on our objective and
flexibility in the means led to the acceptance of our position and to a major arms control achievement.

Negotiators may spend a good deal of time in early
phases in ensuring that they are speaking the same bargaining language. This was the case in the early rounds of both
SALT and the Law of the Sea talks when much time went
into assuring that each side understood what the other
meant in technological terms. In trade negotiations the bargaining language serves to enable negotiators to facilitate
communication and the development of common perceptions about the bargaining environment. Insights into the
formalities of communications are also important for a correct reading of their content. Secretary of State Dean Acheson in his memoirs wrote about a negotiation with the Soviet
Union when knowledge about Russian concessions proved
helpful to him:

> In the summer of 1941 [in the Lend Lease negotiations],
> for days the negotiations went on with exactly the same
> points, often in the same words, made by each side. . . .
> Then I remembered the sound advice Averell Harriman
> had given me some time earlier when he was home from
> Moscow: not to ignore a fundamental fact of Communist
> negotiating procedure—that no Soviet representative
> would ever report home what an opponent *said.* To do so
> would give the impression that he had been impressed
> or was weak or lacked zeal in carrying out his instruc-
> tions. Furthermore unfriendly NKVD men on the dele-
> gation could use any willingness to compromise against
> him. . . .
>   The way to make progress toward some con-
> clusion—even one where no agreement was pos-
> sible—was to recess the meetings for a day or two, sig-

nalling an important consultation, and then to present a paper with some modification of position toward the ultimate acceptable one. This should be followed by another recess to give the Soviet delegation time to communicate with Moscow. The paper would be communicated, since not to do so would be a grave fault. On getting a reply the Soviet negotiator would ask for a resumption of discussion. (Acheson 1969, pp. 85–86)

Signals for Learning

Parties also *learn* from each others' past positions and movements. Each party observes the ways in which the other moves from initial positions, not as a manipulated tactic but as a fixed element of behavior. Knowing how the other party acts or is acting in this case, one can respond properly to obtain the most favorable outcome possible. Thus, observers have frequently noted that Communist negotiators tend to make their concessions late, holding out on fixed positions until the last minute, whereas Americans make concessions early and then hold onto a position judged reasonable to the end. A delegate from the West to the Law of the Sea Conference complained that every Western concession is "banked" by the Third World, to be used as the basis for a new demand when the West has no longer any stock from which to make further concessions. Knowing the other party's behavior patterns allows a negotiator to tailor his behavior to them; he will know what to expect and will not mistake routine behavior for signals of special significance, just as he will be able to interpret the importance of digressions from that routine.

This sense of learning from the other party's behavior so as to know how to respond to it (and even then being caught in one's own wisdom) (Cross 1969), is clearly displayed in an Israeli comment on the Golan Heights negotiations:

Kissinger and, no doubt, the Israelis were never sure what the minimum and maximum Syrian positions were, or what was negotiable and what was not. Thinking at first that the Syrians were following the North Vietnamese model of bargaining, Kissinger pressed Israel to make concessions he considered essential for the continuation of the talks. . . . He found that Syrian concessions were usually forthcoming in order to keep the talks going. . . . Quneitra was of negligible strategic value to Israel but had prestige value for Syria, so Jerusalem was willing to cede the town but bargain hard on its partition first, in order to avoid bargaining on the hills and the entire line. . . . If negotiators reveal in public or in the negotiations their real reasons for accepting an interim agreement, they have given the other side information that can be used against them in future phases of the talks (Aronson 1978, pp. 239–41, 288).

Signals for Teaching

Since parties communicate and learn, they also *teach* each other through their movements. Each party rewards and punishes the responses of the other by its own responses, reacting both to the communications and to the inducements of the other party. It is this combination that is one of the tricky aspects of negotiation: each move is at the same time a position of substance and a "Pavlovian" signal to the other party to stop or continue in the direction already taken. The two may conflict: A party may want to induce the other to continue his concessions but they have nothing more with which to reward his past behavior, or he may want to punish or otherwise deter continuing conduct but may feel that for other reasons concessions are necessary. Nonetheless, parties alter their normal behavior to reinforce the verbal signal that they make or to express matters that cannot be signaled verbally. The Soviet use of ICBM site construction to induce the other side to come to agreement during SALT has already been mentioned. A more complex verbal example in SALT came from the American side: "The delegation did not even use at least one authorized small change—reducing the size of the NCA [National Capitol Area] ABM deployment circle—because of our desire to signal firmness" [Garthoff 1977, p. 14].

Another type of teaching is "leading conduct," in which each concession is met by a raised demand (instead of being rewarded by a lowered demand), much as a gym instructor raises the bar after each successful pole vault. At Geneva, "Mrs. Meir added that the minute Israel offers something or accepts a proposal, Assad just ups his demands," using each previous acceptance as a springboard (Golan 1976, p. 129). An Egyptian official used similar words to describe Israeli negotiating in Jerusalem in December 1977: "We half expected the Israelis to take everything we had to offer and put it in their pockets and ask blandly for more" (*New York Times* December 31, 1977).

Since bidding, communicating, learning, and teaching are all going on at the same time, and sometimes in different directions, the signals are not always clear and the positions are sometimes confused. In addition, some signals may not be directed toward the negotiators in the room at all but to outside parties, a point that will be pursued in the next chapter. However, signals directed toward outside parties may affect the negotiations, for the signal is not credible to the intended audience unless it is pursued with some sincerity, with evidence of receipt by the other side. It is meaningless to ask how much of Panama's and the United States' negotiating behavior in the Panama Canal talks was the "external component" directed toward the gallery in each country, and how much was the "real" negotiating component. The two "components" simply cannot be separated, as if there were a basic price and a gallery surcharge.

Finally, signals cannot be made in any terms one might want, because positions and moves are governed by outside conditions or referents. This last point needs some emphasis here. Many analyses of negotiation assume that parties can make frequent and regular incremental concessions or moves, as if each series of moves had its own innate value and two oranges were simply twice as good as one. Yet it is actually external contexts and considerations that give meaning to details. (For example, the unit may not be oranges at all but the number—say, two—required for a glass of juice, so that five oranges are worth no more than four but six are.) Although the results may be plotted as the convergence of two jagged lines, the actual moves are more like jumping from one criterion or justification for a figure to another (Golan 1976, p. 102). *The detail finally chosen is the consequence of the criterion that justifies it,* not the reverse. It follows, then, that *the prime object in fixing details is to fix the rationale behind them.* If a reason or referent is not established, negotiators end up with purely mechanical determinants such as split-the-difference when it may be harmful to their real interests.

A few cases can be cited as widely differing examples of this phenomenon. Although they will be schematized for discussion, they are necessarily complicated because of the very point being illustrated. In the Spanish–American base negotiations in 1968–70, the Spanish opened with a military aid figure of $1.2 billion; when the United States stuck to its own opener of $100 million, the Spanish rapidly dropped to $745 million, then $700 million, then $400 million, between July and November 1968. The United States then added on a $100 million Export–Import Bank loan, and these two figures, prorated, were included in the one-year interim agreement signed in June 1969. A year later Spain radically revised its dollar demands but maintained the categories, calling for only $20 million in military aid, $125 million in Export–Import Bank loans, and a much larger sum in non-) military aid, for which precise figures are not available. "When this greatly reduced demand [for military aid] was presented to the United States, its offer curve (which had been almost stationary) fell correspondingly," and bargaining shifted to smaller components (in the tens of millions) of nonmilitary aid. Both the final grant total and the final military grant-and-loan total were lower than the highest American offer (Tracy 1978, p. 220).

A second example of concessions resulting from shifting criteria is seen in the establishment of the truce line-in-depth in the 1974–75 disengagement agreements. The initial baseline in the Sinai was the Suez Canal, which was to be some distance from the boundary-in-depth; another possible baseline was centered on the passes partway across the Sinai. The first, informal proposal came from Egyptian General Gamasy at kilometer 101, suggesting staged withdrawals, first to the October 22 lines, next to the Mitla and Gidi passes, and then to an al-Arish–Ras-Muhammad line in the eastern Sinai. The second Egyptian proposal combined stages one and two, suggesting a U.N. zone separating Egyptian lines ten and thirty-five kilometers east of the canal respectively, and demilitarized zones for an unspecified distance behind each of them. The Israeli counterproposal, much later, was for a U.N. zone between the canal and an Israeli withdrawal line ten to twelve kilometers east of the canal (that is, using Gamasy's Egyptian demilitarized zone as the U.N. zone), and partially demilitarized zones for thirty kilometers on either side of the canal. Gamasy's response was less attractive than his previous offer: a U.N. zone between Egyptian and Israeli front lines twenty and thirty-five kilometers east of the canal respectively, and demilitarized zones for ten kilometers behind each of them (Golan 1976, pp. 98, 101, 129).

Disengagement talks were then stopped at kilometer 101 and taken up again in Kissinger's shuttle. President Sadat called for Israeli withdrawal to the Mitla and Gidi passes. Reportedly (Golan 1976, pp. 159–60), Israel debated whether to make a bargaining or a final-line proposal, optii.g for the latter on the basis of Sadat's negotiating style (as opposed to Syrian President Assad's). Israel then reverted to Gamasy's first offer and improved on the Israeli side of it by proposing a U.N. zone between about ten and about twenty kilometers east of the canal, with Egyptian and Israeli demilitarized zones on either side of it. Sadat agreed in principle but disagreed with the application of the principle at the southern part of the line around Suez city; Israeli Defense Minister Dayan is reported to have said, "If I were Sadat, I would not have agreed to a line so close to the Gulf of Suez," and pulled back the line (Golan 1976, p. 161).

Once this agreement in principle was signed, the same process of concessions and referents continued in determining the details of the zones. Artillery was withdrawn to a point where the front lines were out of its range. Israel repeated the same criterion for surface-to-air missiles (SAMs), translated into specific detail as forty kilometers from the opponent's front lines. Egypt, apparently not contesting the criterion, countered that SAM range was actually thirty-five kilometers and anything further than that was a topographically unsuitable site. Israel then countered that emplacements thirty-five kilometers from Israeli lines (fifteen kilometers west of the canal) would endanger the civilian population if fired on and so it was in Egypt's own interest to withdraw further. Egypt accepted, although it is not clear whether it was the unyielding Israeli position or the persuasive Israeli reasoning that won the concession (Golan 1976, pp. 163–64).

As to the military components in the reduced-forces zones, Egypt asked for one and one-half divisions and Israel offered two or three battalions. Referents played a visible role: "Dayan understood the purpose immediately. Divisions come with extra supporting forces such as artillery and engineering units. Battalions do not" (Golan 1976, pp. 162–63). Egypt bowed to the refusal of divisions and demanded ten battalions, Israel proposed eight, and Kissinger persuaded the latter to give in, since another shuttle trip would produce an agreement on nine, and one battalion was scarcely worth the trip. (Similarly, Israel wanted a tank-free zone, and Egypt asked for two hundred, then one hundred, then thirty tanks, which figure was finally accepted. Egypt cited needs of terrain defense and troop morale as justification for the initial demand, although there may have been other criteria that are not known.) Again, judging from the information available on these disengagement examples, the concessions on the lines, zones, and military components were first made in terms of criteria and rationale and then translated into specifics. In other words, there was not simply incremental convergence.

An extreme example comes from the 1971 negotiations on the rent figure for the British use of Malta. Schematically, when a figure was agreed to for some aid category, it was shifted to a different category and used as the basis for a raised demand for the original category. The previous rent was £5 million, three-quarters in grants and one-quarter in loans. Britain offered the same sum but as a grant, plus an additional £3.5 million as a loan, for an £8.5 million total. Malta refused, raised the total by £1 million and Britain agreed. Malta then claimed the new £9.5 million figure as the grant portion alone, not the total, and demanded the £4.8 million development assistance loan in addition. Thereafter, Malta doubled its own bid, asking £19 million in grants. Mediators then proposed a rough split of the difference between the two Maltese figures of £9.5 million (which Britain had meanwhile agreed to) and the £19 million total, for the finally accepted grant figure of £14 million. In the process a similar sum had been extracted from other countries.

A final example, discussed elsewhere (Zartman 1971, pp. 67–74) in full detail, concerns the establishment of the aid sum for the African states associated with the European Common Market. Instead of simply moving toward each other from separate starting points, the six Europeans and the various Africans—sometimes in two groups, sometimes individually—took the total sum apart, shifted from one component to another, seized on different figures to build on (as did Malta), and after a long complex process returned to a total that existed only as the sum of its parts, few of which had been negotiated as discrete items by an arithmetic convergence. Put differently, the final figures arrived at are only understandable through the context of the process of arriving at them, including the choice of criteria as well as figures.

All of the conflicting ingredients outlined above go into the process of finding unique, acceptable details out of a sea of potential agreement points, a process of doing many things with many things at the same time. Any of a number of details could constitute the final agreement and any number of details could be chosen to implement a given formula. The general shape or even the formula for an agreement may be foreseeable by an experienced negotiator or predictable by a skilled analyst, but no such claims can be made about the point where agreement on details will land. *Which detail is chosen depends on how it is chosen.* Or, as Kissinger (1969, p. 212) has said, "The way negotiations are carried out is almost as important as what is negotiated."

The following sections will examine the mechanics of arriving at a common position on details, in an effort to identify when to adopt one kind of move rather than another. As noted, these mechanics can be conceived in different ways—as unilateral tactics, as multilateral interaction, as a structuring of issues. Obviously, it is not possible to state categorically when a particular course of action should be taken. Indeed this probably never will be possible, even when all experience has been catalogued and scientifically analyzed. But, without expecting answers to all situations, one can find guidelines to narrow the leeway otherwise left simply to skill and feel.

MAKING CONCESSIONS

This section examines the role of concessions in negotiations, a matter of great significance, since some concession is necessary in all negotiations. "Concession" refers to the typical image held of negotiation: giving in a little to meet the other fellow's demands. It therefore refers to those negotiations where the stakes can be considered as increments of the same item ("He wants twelve oranges and I want to give him only six," or "He wants twelve dollars for the rug and I want to give him only six dollars"). The ingredients of concession-making are the level at which one opens and the rate at which one concedes. Steady concessions from a moderate position "mean" something different than the same concessions from an outlandish position, in part because the eventual meeting point and the time it takes to get there are widely divergent.

The Need to Concede
"The object of any successful negotiator," according to long-time State Department official Livingston Merchant,

> is knowing in advance what the absolute minimum is
> that you can accept, where you are prepared to walk out
> and have the negotiation fail completely if you can't

maintain your minimum position. And then in the process, in the opening moves of the negotiations, to try to set your position outposts far enough in advance so that you've got concession room if you are backed down to your minimum position by either your Congress or by an Executive department, or by other departments with a certain interest in the negotiating subject, or by your allies. If you are engaged in an alliance negotiation, you are in a much more constricted position from the opening right to the conclusion. (Merchant interview)

Authorities usually maintain that asking for more than one expects to get is the essential strategy of negotiations, disagreeing only on how high to begin and how much to give in. Professor Henry Kissinger (1961) argued (p. 205), "If agreement is usually found between two starting points, there is no point in making moderate offers. Good bargaining technique would suggest a point of departure far more extreme than what one is willing to accept. The more outrageous the initial proposition, the better is the prospect that what one 'really' wants will be considered a compromise." Things may not be quite as simple as that in practice and the debate continues, in part because the secretary of state did not follow the rules suggested by the professor.

A former Arms Control Agency administrator and professor of diplomacy, Fred Iklé, argued before Congress:

All too frequently the positions of the Communist powers are viewed as immutable. During the formulation of the United States' negotiating position within the State Department and in inter-agency discussion in Washington, it happens often that a possible American proposal or a Western demand is voted down as being "unacceptable" to the opponent. Our negotiators and policy planners in fact make them so. Since the positions of Communist governments, much as our own, tend to change only gradually under the influence of negotiation our abstaining from "unacceptable" demands denies us a possibility of modifying a Communist position.

A member of the SALT delegation, William Van Cleave, testified:

The Soviet approach included positions that the Soviets must have expected to be nonnegotiable. These extreme positions could then be used to cause change in the United States' positions or they could be removed at any time as a major concession. The Soviets may have been surprised at the way that some of these "nonnegotiable positions" (for example in FBS and ACA defense) eventually became negotiable but quite possibly they thoroughly anticipated it.

The results achieved by different kinds of concession behavior add up, like so many things in negotiation, to a paradox. Unilateral "cooperation begets cooperation; . . . noncooperation begets noncooperation" (Bartos 1974, p. 270). Noncooperative behavior leads to more favorable outcomes if successful but also runs a high risk of rupture (Zartman 1971, p. 221). The arguments in favor of each strategy are not surprising. Cooperative behavior—opening reasonably, offering concessions, and extending trust—creates a trusting, reasonable image of oneself and conveys a trustworthy, strong image of the other party. It creates a positive atmosphere of understanding and creativity (Ibid., pp. 263–78). Studies have shown that the United States responded positively to the Soviets in this way in the Cuban missile negotiations (Jensen 1976, pp. 300–02, Hopmann and Smith 1978, p. 171). But cooperative behavior also signals that the cooperative party cares less about his outcome than about the process, and suggests that he invites exploitation. Although he may want to project himself as positive and fair, he may in fact end up appearing as a pushover and a patsy.

Noncooperative behavior—extreme openers, few concessions, taking advantage of the other whenever possible—may in fact induce respect and create an image of shrewdness for a negotiator, behavior the negotiator would probably prefer his opposite number not emulate. Noncooperative behavior creates a defensive and conflictual atmosphere, but it shows that the negotiator is nobody's fool. If the other side wants an agreement it will have to come to terms. The United States reacted in this way in the Cuban missile negotiations, at the time when the Soviets were acting tough and unfriendly. Said Robert Kennedy, "We will have to make a deal at the end, but we must stand absolutely firm now. Concessions must come at the end of negotiations, not at the beginning" (Schlesinger 1965, p. 811). At best—as in the Cuban missile crisis—the whole cycle is a teaching–learning process, as well as a simple reaction. Negotiators say, "Smile and we'll smile with you, right down to an agreement, but frown and we'll frown too, and neither of us will get anywhere, except to blows."

Philip Jessup, who was an ambassador-at-large during Truman's presidency, and U.S. permanent representative to the United Nations, recalled that a tough, uncompromising stand was necessary for the United States in its negotiations with the Dutch on the Indonesian question: "Aside from the disagreements inside the Department of State it did seem best to be very firm in saying, 'You are not going to get anywhere this way with your armed forces, and you've really got to meet the demands of the Nationalists.' I think that was necessary. If we had been softer on that I think the Dutch would have been even more recalcitrant" (Jessup interview).

However, for each approach, overdoing is its undoing. Cooperators carrying the tactic to extremes may mistake cooperation for an end, become overly flexible, and give up

too much while noncooperators may mistake noncooperation for an end, become overly rigid, and fail to get an
agreement. As a result, in a pattern that will be examined
more thoroughly in the next section, we find an apparent
contradiction of the initial statement on cooperation:
"Toughness . . . generates softness; softness generates toughness," assuming an overriding desire for agreement. A party
which shows itself cooperative may create an agreeable atmosphere but the other party tends to stiffen its demands,
whereas a party which shows itself unyielding forces the
other to give in if it wants an agreement. Studies suggest that
this was the pattern of American behavior in the Test-Ban
Treaty negotiations: Americans tended to toughen their
negotiating stands when they perceived the Soviets in more
positive terms, while relaxing their stands when they perceived the Soviets as tougher. Soviet behavior was the reverse, although not as strongly marked (Hopmann and Smith
1978, p. 171).

The argument for toughness also weighs against even
considering fallback positions in the detailed bargaining
phase. Refusal to consider alternatives is a form of commitment, like burning bridges, and has been used, at least by the
central authority over the negotiating team. SALT again provides a good example. "The White House had two purposes
in denying the delegation a fallback position. First, it
wanted to create an aura of 'hanging tough on SLBMs,' as
one participant put it, since Moscow still doubted Washington's strength of purpose on this issue. Second, it feared
another leak . . . and wanted no fallback positions committed
to paper" (Garthoff 1977, p. 18).

The Way to Concede

There is something to be learned from this cycle of
findings, even though taken as a whole it is circular and
banal. Each strategy has its logic. There is a time for co-

operative behavior, and such behavior conveys certain, if conflicting, signals to the other party. There are other times for tough behavior, whose signals are less ambiguous but whose outcome involves high risk for high gain. Together, the two constitute a teaching–learning cycle. Since negotiations are not games of fun or games of chance, *negotiators should adopt tactics that maximize both the amount and the chances of gain, or in other words, pick a mixed strategy.* The mix can be accomplished in time or in issues, maximizing the flexibility available to negotiators. Parties will be tough on the issues of greatest importance to them, but can use this toughness to generate concessions and then reward and reciprocate with their own concessions on other matters. Thus, in general, negotiators should be tough to demand and soft to reward.

The best mixed strategy involves a high opener, few concessions until a final one for agreement, and the inducement of trust by other means. A high—although not extreme— opening position slightly higher than expectations of the final outcome permits both a clear statement of the alternative, with its justification, and some room for maneuvering. An unyielding stand on that position maximizes the gains of negotiation and communicates a sense of justness and necessity about the position. It also avoids the grinding down that multiple concessions invite, for there is no doubt that *the more incremental concessions are made, the more are expected.* That is why parties try to make any concessions a once-and-for-all jump to an acceptable agreement. Negotiations work best when the parties have become so familiar with the facts of the situation and the values of the other party that they can, on the first jump, propose a solution that will be acceptable. In the absence of such sure aim, one can also explore the possibility of final concessions in other ways—by making a concession contingent on final overall agreement, by shifting the debate to the type of concession the other would accept and then grinding that down, by making a concession on a "final offer" basis (Newhouse 1973, pp. 251, 255). The greater the role of contingent agreements in the negotiations, the more important trust becomes. Yet, again paradoxically, the more the whole structure of the agreement depends on an interlocking arrangement of contingent elements, the more the need to trust becomes built into the agreement. If some of these contingencies can be called in during the negotiations, the element of trust is strengthened.

Other Ways to Concede

Admittedly, a strategy of high opener and few concessions may not be possible. When one party, after properly holding out on his high position and trying to create an atmosphere of trust, presents his revised position as a final offer, the other party may flatly reject it and call for a new concessionary position, or may accept it as a basis for further demands and concessions, or may try to whittle it down without either accepting or rejecting, or may try to maximize his own gain by accepting a concession that in fact was not offered.

Robert Lovett warned of the care needed in offering contingent concessions:

> In a labor negotiation—and some of the ones that I have seen have been very bitter—you can't take back what you put on the table yesterday, so you need to be very careful before you put a concession on the table. You say, "All right, we'll give you a five dollar raise on the assumption that you will do this and that and the other thing." The other fellow says, "No, I'll take the five dollar raise, but I'll be damned if I do that." (Lovett interview)

Each side may then try to hold onto its position for as long as possible, knowing that, although there is further give in both positions, the other side may be impatient and give in first. When the revised position is presented as final offer, the other side may be prepared to still sit tight. The "eyeballing" moment has been reached. What started out as a mixed but firm strategy rapidly turns into a soft strategy faced with toughness for one party.

There are no conclusive answers on how to avoid this. One partial answer would be to *prolong the original process,* putting time into preparation of the "final offer" and avoiding the impression that it is a jump made lightly and easily repeated. Another, more drastic, is *the sibylline tactic of withdrawing the concession and raising the demands* if the "final offer" is not accepted, although such tactics can often lead to a hardening of positions on the other side. Third, the party may simply *make no more offers* but encourage and induce the other party to make and then modify his own proposals. Finally, the party may *head back toward the formula phase,* in part or in whole, and put together a new proposal in entirely different terms.

To arrive at agreement on details there are other types of approaches to concession-making than the mixed strategy. At least three distinct alternatives appear, and there may be variants. One is the standard concessionary tactic, in which the party starts high and makes frequent concessions until the other finally agrees. Although in theory it is easy to imagine the position descending until it reaches the other party's fixed threshold of acceptability, in reality that threshold is not fixed at all. When the other party sees the opponent readily making concessions, it raises its threshold of acceptability to wring the largest concessions out of the opponent. This "soft" tactic has been used by weaker parties with high needs, little power to force concessions, and mainly moral appeals to rely on, such as developing nations, at least until the OPEC era brought a radical change. In such circumstances for non-OPEC nations, it may well be the most successful. The accelerated concessionary tactic is suitable when it is the best one can do; at least, it creates a sense of obligation on the other side. But, almost by definition, it yields low results compared with one and often both parties' initial positions.

Second is the high unyielding position with a jump to agreement at the end. Such a position either assumes that agreement is only worthwhile at a certain fixed point, since the security position is not very costly, or it assumes that negotiations can continue a long time, until the other party agrees, since it has no time costs. Usually, too, there is a moral stand attached to this position, enabling the party to hold out even when it hurts. Revolutionary and, lately, developing countries often adopt this tactic, benefiting from a sense of righteousness in conditions where things cannot get much worse and there is nothing to lose, and sometimes strengthened by some power base which can be used against the opponents. Qaddafi started the oil price rises of the 1970s at the beginning of the decade essentially on the belief that "people such as the Libyans who have lived for 5000 years without petroleum can live without it even for scores of years in order to reach their legitimate rights" (Schuler 1976, p. 125). This "tough" tactic raises the level of the outcome when it works, but it is risky, increasing the chances of breakdown and bitterness and adding often useless delays.

Third, a party may pick a position that it feels, after study, is equitable to all sides and stick to it, in effect playing the role of mediator in its own case (Ramberg 1978, pp. 137–38). Such a position shows an arrogance in stepping out of role that only the very powerful and the very just can afford to display. Yet states do practice it, for there is something both appealing and expeditious in identifying the outcome without wasting time on a process of getting there. The tactic sometimes works, but frequently the other party confuses the choice of the tactic with a self-serving solution in disguise. Or else it leads to minimal agreement on the basis of the lowest common denominator between the parties' interests, leaving more difficult, significant, and innovative solutions beyond the scope of the approach (Frye 1974, p. 84). Commentators have charged that the Soviets or both sides played this strategy in the SALT I and test ban negotiations to arrive at a very limited agreement or to waste time in the process.

When the parties do make concessions they may attempt to maximize them in the eyes of the other side: "I am conceding this point for the sake of this negotiation, although they will not be happy at home with this." "This is worth a lot to me." To avoid having the other side perceive a concession as weakness, a party may claim that it is conceding only because it expects its opposite number to do so in the future, or that its concession is conditional on a quid pro quo (Jervis 1970, p. 198). While attempting to maximize its concessions, a party may try to minimize the offers of the other side (Lall 1966, p. 299). All these embellishments on tactics often make it hard to identify the real strategy of the other side in choosing its combination of large and small concessions.

EXCHANGING POINTS

The previous discussion concentrated on situations where the parties resolved differences of detail on a single issue by moving toward each other. Such situations are not the most frequent. More commonly there are many issues, and concessions are made among them in order to arrive at detailed points of agreement. It is in this context that Homans's maxim comes into play most specifically, for *the secret of detailed negotiation is to exchange "goods valued more by one party than they cost the other and goods valued more by the other party than they cost the first"* (Homans 1961, p. 62). This is the principle underlying the most satisfactory agreements, although of course things cannot always be so simple as a double-column list of exchangeable goods might suggest. Some things may be valued by both parties, and sometimes a party cares even more about denying an item to the other than having it for himself. However, humans need to be convinced of the rightness of their actions by some criteria, and simply deciding given details in the other's favor because he agreed to decide some in our direction is scarcely a justification that would stand up in the court of public debate. Such exchanges must at least be balanced, and at best balanced in each party's favor in his own eyes. Therefore, details may be arranged in such a way that all parties get most of what they want, but they must also be justified—some might say rationalized—by some defensible criteria. This takes the argument back to the discussion of formulas, for broad justifications which cover a number of details are stronger—less controvertible—than individual justifications for each item. The latter are not rare, however, since even a good formula may not be able to determine the disposition of all details.

For example, a formula may be applied on a number of different levels. To the Israelis, "territory for security" translated as "the depth of withdrawal is to be determined by the degree of normalization."

Israel also mentioned a much more advanced arrangement than such a limited "substitute for peace" as "open bridges": a final, "peacelike" arrangement in exchange for a withdrawal from most of Sinai. Failing that Israel offered a smaller withdrawal in exchange for a binding declaration of nonbelligerency for a period of seven to twelve years. Another alternative Jerusalem suggested was a political arrangement that would not end the state of war but would keep war from breaking out for a reasonable length of time; territorial concessions in this case would be quite small. The second of the twelve points was Egypt's response to these proposals: the passes and the oilfields for a declaration that the conflict would be resolved by peaceful means. . . . The Israelis saw it as no gain if it remained general and divorced from a time commitment. (Aronson 1978, pp. 278–79)

Thus the second Sinai disengagement negotiations were an effort to find the appropriate items of exchange under the agreed formula. However, sometimes such exchanges are not merely drawn from different levels of values lined up in two columns under the formula, but from two unrelated pools of times which are simply valued more by each party. In the final negotiations for the limited test-ban treaty in July 1963, the Soviet Union conceded to a principled U.S. objection to banning nuclear weapons for self-defense, then to the U.S. insistence on the principle of a withdrawal clause, then to U.S. objections in principle to linkage to a nonaggression pact; in exchange the United States conceded to a Russian objection in principle to the peaceful use of nuclear explosions (Whelan 1979, pp. 378–80). Exchange of concessions made the agreement possible, but the concessions were compatible with although not directly derived from the formula.

The opening of formal discussions in the Geneva Conference on Indochina in 1954 was delayed by the question of who was to be represented at the conference table. Molotov, representing the Soviet delegation, demanded that a Vietminh delegation participate in the talks. Anthony Eden (1960, p. 130) wrote that this could not be resisted, and agreed with Bidault that in accepting it they should receive a pledge of Communist cooperation in the evacuation of wounded from Dien Bien Phu. Molotov and Chou En-lai both refused, but in behind-the-scenes talks an unofficial arrangement was worked out whereby when Vietminh participation was announced, the other side's willingness to help with the evacuation of prisoners was also agreed to. After this exchange the negotiators could then move on to the big issue.

Even when ostensibly only one issue is under discussion it is usually broken down into components, each of which requires agreement in detail; also, breaking down an issue into pieces that allow for the mutual exchange is often the easiest way to achieve agreement. As a rule, *if agreement cannot be reached on an issue, negotiators should break it down into its components and seek agreement on them.*

Breaking down an issue is a challenge to perception and imagination, for the pieces must be so defined as to be susceptible to resolution. Fractioning alone is not enough; fractions must be composed in such a way as not to constitute irreducible stumbling blocks to agreement (cf. Fisher 1969). Such action allows resolution not by mutual concession but by exchange of concessions, in which a party gives in on some points in exchange for the second party's agreement with his position on other points. Breaking a rock down into smaller pieces, as one negotiator termed it, may keep the negotiations from stumbling by preventing discussions on vague and nonexistent wholes or on different parts of the issue without negotiators being aware of it. The Dutch negotiators dealing with the South Moluccan kidnappers in the spring of 1977 turned their efforts from surrender of the hijackers to conditions for the release of one group of hostages after another. The new approach was more successful than the previous one; but like any step-by-step or piece-by-piece strategy—notably that in the Middle East—the negotiator has to be careful not to pay the whole wallet for one item. Breaking up the issue of the Gidi and Mitla passes into their territorial and security components allowed for a trade-off that permitted agreement, in the second Sinai disengagement. in SALT II, among many other compromises, "the United States was ready to agree to the higher overall [ICBM] figure favored by the Russians if they agreed to a separate ceiling of 1,200 for multiple warhead vehicles [MIRVs]" (*New York Times*, May 4, 1978).

ARRANGING DETAILS

The Time for Complexity

Handling details one by one and playing them off against each other are two ways of making the problem more amenable to a solution. If one does not work the other should be tried. But when should one make a bundle of the items being settled and when should they be handled point by point? When should side issues and side payments be added and when should the negotiator dig in his heels and fight it out on the issue? Experiments tend to show that packaged issues take longer to resolve then individual issues but if they are packaged into bundles that "belong" together, they provide a greater opportunity for flexibility and creativeness and a greater chance to avoid a winner-take-all situation and to provide for a balanced distribution of payoffs as an incentive to general agreement (Rubin and Brown 1975, pp. 145, 147, 151, 155).

Experience tends to confirm these rules: *When issues can be grouped in a natural package that provides balanced payoffs, they should first be handled as a package;* when a few individual components of the package resist group treatment, they may need individual treatment or possibly postponement. Later, as other details fall into place, it may be possible to return the recalcitrant issue to the package again. Particularly with very complex negotiations involving many issues and many parties, it is often necessary to table positions, decompose them, and aggregate the relevant information to explore incrementally the interface of bargaining positions (Winham 1976, p. 13). This process in itself may take a very long time, as the lengthy Law of the Sea sessions (and intersessions) have shown.

One negotiator who participated in the early rounds of SALT contrasted the Soviet approach of seeking general agreement in principle prior to disclosing any specifics of their proposals with the American approach of advancing a fairly complete, complex, and detailed package. It was important for the American team to make clear that the trade-offs and tie-ins were inseparably linked, in order to prevent the other side from picking out only those items it favored. The United States therefore provided the stipulation that until everything was agreed nothing was agreed (Garthoff 1977, p. 22).

Side payments and inducements add another element of complexity. First of all, the side payments must be closely related to the item under discussion. It is hard to make a party swallow a repugnant detail with a completely unrelated inducement; what he needs is something that will expunge the repugnancy of the detail itself. Yet promises and threats do come into play when relevant arguments in favor of a point of detail fail. In Sinai II in 1975, only large American side payments in aid and promises provided Israel with the balanced exchange that it needed. Furthermore, it frequently happens that although both parties' justifications of their separate stands are perfectly valid, one argument simply does not "take" the other in its proponent's own terms. Israel is only eight miles wide and has a right to security, but the Palestinians have a right to their own state. When neither argument is in trumps, compensations and inducements can sometimes be used to change the terms of argument.

Voluntary inducements come as either threats or promises, although the two are related. A threat, after all, is only an implicit promise stating that, if the other party will come to terms, we will promise to stop doing something unpleasant that we would threaten to do if the other did not comply.

The difference between the two lies in the fact that, in the threat, the negotiating party itself is imposing the unpleasant sanction, while in the promise the unpleasant situation exists and the negotiating party is offering a pleasant sanction. General findings on the two contingent sanctions are again contradictory (were they not, one would clearly stand out over the other and the use of the proper sanctions would not be such a delicate decision) (Rubin and Brown 1975, pp. 280, 283, 285–86). Threats and promises tend to be last resorts in bargaining, but they do increase the incidence of compliance and concession. Threats sour the atmosphere and over the long run reduce the likelihood of a mutually favorable agreement. Promises generally cost more to implement than threats, since they are usually permanent contingencies. But to the extent that threats tend to be more effective than promises they are useful in obtaining a minimum necessary agreement, whereas creative and ameliorative agreements are more appropriately the subject of promises. Finally, for all their specific effectiveness, promises and threats can become further subjects of negotiations, multiplying rather than simplifying the points of disagreement.

The choice among threats and promises in general is primarily a matter of cost and credibility. The maker wants an inducement that is as cheap and as effective as possible, two contradictory criteria in many cases. But since threats and promises are contingent sanctions they must be credible, and to be credible they must—among other things—be in proportion to the desired goal.

When the Trieste negotiations had stalled on the issue of the last few square miles of territory, President Eisenhower intervened in a personal letter to President Tito, writing: "As a military man, you will understand that if the Trieste problem is settled, it will be possible to create a greater power toward defense in that area than if the Trieste question is not settled; and American assistance can therefore be spent with maximum effectiveness only if a settlement is achieved" (Campbell 1976, p. 169). That promise, offered by a president of the United States who had been a wartime hero, changed the situation, in the view of the Yugoslav negotiator Vladimir Velebit (Ibid., p. 92).

Threats to bomb and promises to aid are credible inducements for lesser details but not for large issues of substance. Furthermore, threats and promises can be twice called as bluffs: the other party can dare the maker to implement a threat, and he can then refuse to comply once the sanction is made good. Similarly, a party can challenge the other to come through on a promise, and then can renege on its agreement to comply. Once called, the inducements are useless. Military and political diplomats who want to induce with armaments sold or dropped or with foreign aid payments frequently forget this, and hear the other side ask, "What more can you do against me or what have you done for me lately?" Thus, the United States was pulled into ineffective escalations in the 1960s in Vietnam, and the Begin government let itself be drawn into an increasingly violent response in 1979–80 against the Palestinians, as the French had against the Algerians in the 1950s. In the Vietnam negotiations in the early 1970s, the promise of postwar aid was brought up by the United States: North Vietnam rejected the package of which it was part but retained the item as reparations and made sure it was included in the final agreement (although never implemented).

The Time for Ambiguity

The matter of precision versus ambiguity is also relevant to resolving details. Diplomatic writers generally agree that precision is important; imprecise agreements run into trouble later. What they point out less frequently is that calculated—or as Kissinger termed it, "constructive"—ambiguity is often very useful. Careful sidestepping of a delicate issue on which no agreement is possible, and deliberately equivocal wording, have each saved the day on more than one occasion. The Yaounde Association agreement between Africa and the EEC avoided useless debate over its legal basis by grounding itself on the principles of the Rome Treaty without specifying which ones; the 1967 Security Council resolution on the Middle East conflict referred to "secure frontiers" and Resolution 242 called for "return of occupied territories"; the 1964 joint declaration which began Panama Canal negotiations referred to "procedures" but not to "canal," "negotiations," or "treaty." These three examples of understandings that cleared the way for negotiations illustrate how such ambiguities can be particularly constructively used. But an avoidance of the specific can also be useful in the case of terminal agreements. If the rest of the details all fall into place, one point of disagreement should not be allowed to hold up the accord. At this point, "understandings"—as calculated ambiguities may be termed—can be useful. Terminal ambiguities may be successfully combined with a procedural mechanism to solve presently unresolved cases as they later arise. The initial advice still stands, however: precise agreement is important; only in exceptional cases should ambiguity be used, and then only consciously.

A device akin to procedural formula is also helpful at the end of negotiations. When disagreement on procedural details prevents the conclusion of negotiations, negotiators look for a phrase that is broad enough to cover both positions without being so ambiguous as to be meaningless, as in the following example. Theodore Achilles was on the United States delegation to the negotiation that drew up the NATO Charter. There was a disagreement among the parties on how long the treaty should last. The French were the most anxious to see the treaty concluded, he recalled, and they were pressing for a fifty-year duration for the treaty. "We doubted that the Senate would approve a binding U.S. commitment for anywhere near that long," he said. "We argued that out for a long time and finally compromised on the actual formula: an indefinite duration with anybody being able to withdraw after the treaty had been in effect for twenty years. The French threatened not to sign unless it was a fifty-year duration; but we knew they wanted the treaty the most" (Achilles interview).

Not only should negotiations be precise on details: they should also be complete and comprehensive. It may be easier to limit discussion of details to those on which parties can agree, but the unresolved issues will return to haunt the parties (or their successors). This is a different matter than the omissions of the formula stage, where negotiators set out to define the part of the problem they will tackle, avoiding the rest. Once this decision is made, all the details within the problem so defined should be examined. Negotiation as a form of conflict resolution and problem-solving means that participants should draw up an agreement that fills out the natural dimensions of the problem or conflict. It means that they must identify, anticipate, and even invent if necessary all the conflictual aspects of the issue and either resolve them or—again—provide procedures for resolving them (in specific or, more likely, in general) in the future. If in the end, after these conflictual ramifications have been brought to light, the parties together or individually decide to leave a particularly difficult detail unresolved or covered by an ambiguous "understanding," it should be done exceptionally and deliberately, and not passed by unwittingly.

The Time for Momentum

The fact that both parties have agreed to explore the possibility of negotiating in no way assures that the climate for opening talks will be friendly and conducive to problem-

a turning point that both relates to and alters the value of
the questions under discussion. At some point during the
bargaining a "crest" occurs, after which the rest of the items
are rapidly resolved and the general feeling is one of being in
the "home stretch." This crest may be described in various
ways: it is the point where enough is agreed upon to constitute an acceptable accord even if the remaining points are
unresolved, or the point where enough is agreed on favorably to outweigh any remaining disagreements or nonagree-
ments. It would be too much to say that after the crest remaining points do not matter, but it would not be inaccurate
to say that, at that point, the agreement itself becomes a
positive good in the eyes of the parties, to be defended
against loss just like the other demands of the parties. After
the details of the limited test ban treaty had been hammered
out by Great Britain, the United States and the Soviet Union,
neither side wanted the treaty impeded by problems involving accession by states like East Germany or the People's
Republic of China, unrecognized by the United States at that
time. Therefore, they made all three signatory governments
depositories instead of the customary one, so that East Germany could sign and yet not claim recognition by the United
States (Jacobson and Stein 1966, p. 458).

On December 5, 1979, Lord Carrington announced that
the Patriotic Front had accepted the broad outlines of Britain's cease-fire proposals in the final phase of the Lancaster
House negotiations on the future of Zimbabwe, after having
previously agreed to a new constitution and arrangements
for the transition from war to all-party elections. "What we
have got to do now is to tie up the details, and they oughtn't
to take very long," Lord Carrington said. "With good will,
and I am sure that after today there is good will, we ought to
be able to tie up the details in a few days" (*New York Times*,
December 6, 1979). Despite the fact that the details of the
timing of the cease-fire and the number of assembly points

solving. Indeed the very opposite is often the case, particularly if bitter disputes have dragged on for a long time. In a
hostile climate, reconciling and then combining different
conceptions of an issue may be difficult if not impossible,
whatever the objective possibilities. The parties often find it
useful to seek agreement on certain details at the outset—
even at the beginning of the formula phase—to improve the
climate of the negotiations, since hard bargaining and
breakdowns in the negotiations lie ahead as the tougher issues of substance are approached. Creating an atmosphere
for agreement at an early stage by dealing with procedural
details or other minor points may be very useful. Joseph E.
Johnson, who was on the U.S. delegation to the San Francisco Conference that drew up the United Nations Charter,
explains: "One cannot long negotiate or observe negotiations without noting the importance of the earliest stages.
There is a psychological value in getting the two sides in the
right sort of mood by taking easy questions, discussing them
and reaching agreement—however inconsequential the
questions may be. In many, though not all cases, this type of
exercise can be curiously useful in creating a climate"
(Johnson interview).

Negotiations soon come to have an internal dynamic that
many negotiators have described as bargaining rhythm.
Rather than a steady flow of concessions, the bargaining
rhythm may include long periods without movement while
both sides stand pat. This does not mean that they plan no
further concessions, but rather that they are trying to sound
out and wear down the other side. A negotiator should be
prepared for the tedious aspects of his job. Many negotiations will not move rapidly and the frustrations of dealing
with an opposite number who refuses to do what seems perfectly justifiable and productive in terms of a final agreement
mount as the negotiations drag on. Disrupting the process of
bargaining may be a tactic to throw the other side off bal-

ance. Kenneth Young (1968), writing of the negotiating style of the People's Republic of China under Mao, saw it as calculated to induce tension and disrupt momentum, coupled with an unwillingness to consider smaller issues on the way toward resolution of larger issues (Young 1968, p. 15). Arthur Dean, among many others, felt that the Russians exploited the tedium of the bargaining rhythm, leading to precipitous exasperation. Although the North Koreans' use of the tactic in the early 1950s provides the best example, Dean's examples came from the test ban negotiations: "Overeagerness only plays into Communist hands. It pays to listen, to be precise, determined, and willing to spend time, without any sign of being impatient, angry, or annoyed" (pp. 44–45). Alexis Johnson and Gerard Smith, commenting on SALT, have felt that the typically American contribution to the tedium of bargaining comes from a sometimes exaggerated emphasis on details, technicalities, fine print, and loophole closing (Smith 1977, pp. 18–19; Whelan 1979, pp. 458–59). Referring to the whole process, Johnson explained, "You must compare it to the matter of how a porcupine makes love: very, very carefully" (Whelan 1979, p. 458).

Component issues of the negotiating problem usually come in assorted sizes, both of difficulty and of importance. Usually there are one or more issues of overwhelming importance to the solution of the problem, and the moment at which these are taken up is crucial to the success of the negotiations in general. Sometime soon after the resolution of a few minor issues to test the seriousness of the parties and after the agreement on a formula, the moment comes to tackle the details of *the big issue*. The formula for agreement must encompass the big issue, but its actual resolution in detail may be prepared through agreement on smaller issues first. In the view of George McGhee, a former State Department officer,

It's good to identify clearly the big but not to attempt to solve them would bring an end to the negotia and go around them and work out and come back to them. But you mu that everyone knows what they are, ar mind. If you can't tackle them immedi ary problems, the solution for which m to accomplish the big ones. (McGhee i

If the big issue is tackled too early ther on the record to facilitate agreement. If, or the big issue is raised too late, potential tra have no value and negotiators may be exha problems before ever reaching the big on Brown 1975, p. 148; Iklé 1964, chap. 11; Ke hardest test of the formula is obviously the once it is settled in detail, important momen created for the resolution of lesser issues and been established to hold the formula in place the big issue is reached, however, momentu been built up toward agreement and the neg have a psychological and political stake in rea tlement. The Trieste negotiations showed the im the timing of consideration of the major issue. A both Italian and Yugoslav negotiators talked o agreement on side issues; however, it was clear th agreement on the big issue—the matter of territ session—the whole agreement would unravel (1976, p. 16).

Much of the detail phase (phase three) deals subtle balancing of important and unimportant de addition to their innate importance, details change v cording to the moment in the process of negotiation a they are handled. The resolution of details is usually r

where the guerrillas would be required to gather before voting were extremely difficult, and even required a last-minute British concession on the number of assembly points to win agreement, by that time both sides had an overwhelming stake in seeing the agreement completed.

In his account of the Geneva negotiations to end the conflict in Indochina, Eden recalls that agreement was quickly reached on the principle that the parties would work for a military armistice before discussing details of a political settlement. The negotiations stalled on the issue of Laos and Cambodia, which the other side wanted to include in a blanket settlement. That issue was temporarily bypassed and the parties went on to discuss the composition of an international control commission to supervise the armistice. They deadlocked on this issue as well. The negotiations were under some pressure as the Americans were apprehensive that the French and Vietminh would make an agreement on their own. On June 15, when the negotiations seemed nearer to breakdown than ever before, Eisenhower instructed the U.S. delegation to bring the negotiations to an end. On June 17, Foreign Minister Bidault and Chou En-lai proposed holding separate military staff talks on Laos and Cambodia; if accepted, this would enable talks to begin with all three Indochina states. The next day the Chinese proposed that the supervisory commission be comprised of India, Canada, and Poland, which was accepted. Eden (1960, p. 159) recalls, "From that moment the tangled ends of the negotiations began to sort themselves out."

It is no paradox that the greatest chance of rupture comes after the crest. Since at this point there is already enough agreement to outweigh remaining disagreements, and since each party can count on the other's interest in seeing the agreement carried through, the post-crest phase is the time when the parties can try to slip in some preferred position or even undo an earlier point of agreement. This is the parties' last chance to test and even to make a final attempt to change the agreement thus far achieved, since thereafter it will be too late. Each party can figure that the other side will not risk the entire agreement just for one lesser point of disagreement, and so a few advantages can be won without danger of refusal.

President Nixon was a master in the use of the crest. After the November 1969 summit with Premier Sato of Japan on the principles of an Okinawa agreement, Nixon, Kissinger, and Sato met in the anteroom of the Oval Office for a "necessary private agreement related informally to" Okinawa on the outstanding textile problems between the two countries (Morris 1977, p. 104). Newhouse (1973, pp. 249, 255) captured well the problem of seizing the crest in describing the final days of strategic arms limitation talks at the Moscow summit phase of 1972.

> A number of agreements were reached, most of which had been worked out in advance. An exception was SALT, the main event. Unlike a political convention, which, however divided, will ultimately agree on a candidate, it was only probable, not inevitable (as most people thought), that the Moscow talks would produce a SALT agreement. The affair nearly foundered on the SLBM [submarine-launched ballistic missile] replacement issue. . . . They were eyeball to eyeball, as Dean Rusk might have put it; Nixon refused to budge and seemed prepared to accept the consequences. Brezhnev must have perceived this, and he was apparently less prepared to accept the anticlimax of a failure on SALT . . . at that point, "it began to break."

The need to include necessary but difficult details, the sense of the "home stretch" accompanied by the heightened chance of being called "out" anyhow, and the ability to accept failure as the relevant form of power are all illustrated in this incident.

BRINGING NEGOTIATIONS TO AN END

Negotiations end when there is agreement on the outstanding issues. This can come when parties have exchanged agreements on each other's positions or when, through concessions or through joint discovery of implementing details, they have both moved to a point which they feel is the best they can do under the circumstances. Agreement can come about simply through a full working schedule that has carefully considered all the angles and resolved all possible points of dispute. In other words, "the best they can do" can be either a substantive or a procedural solution. It may refer substantively to a "Pareto optimal point," the most any party can get without depriving the other party of anything, or a solution which is fairest for everyone by whatever the definition of justice has been. It may also refer procedurally to "do" rather than to "best." If a compromise on details has been carefully worked out, each concession brought with a concession in the other direction, each point packaged in exchange with another, it may simply not be possible to add on additional points, statements, or advantages, even if they do not come out of the other party's share. The parties have defined the best they can do in reality, although what was feasible may not be the theoretical best or Pareto optimum.

But since—as Iklé has reminded us—the negotiator is always faced with a threefold choice of agreeing, refusing agreement, and continuing to talk to improve the terms of agreement, there must be some kind of constraint to keep the negotiators from continually picking the third alternative. Even in the above cases of naturally working out agreement, there must be some sense of time costs, the costs or losses associated with delays in agreement. Again, as Cross has reminded us, "If it does not matter when you agree, it does not matter whether you agree."

The commonest way of formalizing time costs and of

providing an external constraint is through the *deadline*. A deadline is actually a jointly imposed or recognized ultimatum. It works in many ways. It tells when time costs will suddenly rise or begin, by fixing a sanction to go into effect when a certain period of negotiation has elapsed. It sets a time when the parties' security position will materialize, when the alternative to a negotiated agreement will suddenly become a reality. Therefore it also sets the moment before which the parties will have to make their final proposals, proposals that the deadline converts, without necessarily requiring any explicit wording, into a take-it-or-leave-it offer. For if the negotiator usually has Iklé's threefold choice available, proposals offered at the last minute, just before the deadline, become proposals on which the third alternative of further discussion is no longer practical. The negotiator is left with the necessity of choosing between accepting agreement and refusing agreement, and of weighing both against the consequences of non-agreement, when the sanctions and security positions come into effect. Thus parties may actually be worse off with no agreement after negotiations have failed than before they started, which explains why they may accept a last-minute offer that they would have refused earlier.

There are two kinds of deadlines—those set by the parties or party, and those imposed from the outside. Even when there is no explicitly fixed deadline from inside, one often exists nonetheless; parties have a sense of when an agreement is expected, hotel reservations for the delegations are made for an estimated period, and frequently an unrelated date such as summer or year-end (Christmas) vacation, some other conference, a summit meeting, an election, or an opening date for parliament, serves as an implicit deadline. "We must get an agreement nailed down by the end of the year or the problem will continue to drag on until the next U.N. session," is the kind of statement that implies a deadline in the absence of a formal one.

In the SALT I negotiations and the Okinawa negotiations, a deadline was provided by the scheduling of a summit meeting between Russian and American and Japanese and American heads of government, respectively. President Nixon in each case wanted to announce an agreement. John Hickerson, a former Assistant Secretary of State, recalled how Secretary of State James Byrnes had committed a serious error during negotiations in Moscow in 1945 by letting slip that he had commitments in the United States just before Christmas: "I remember when I read that telegram reporting that I threw up my hands and said, 'There goes the ballgame.' Nothing happened until the very last minute, and then a whole host of little things happened" (Hickerson interview). When Pierre Mendes-France, as the new French premier, gave himself thirty days to arrive at an agreement at Geneva on Indochina, it was predictable that the agreement would not take place before the twenty-ninth day, and in fact it did occur only on the thirty-second. When President Carter set the deadline for an agreement with Iran on the release of the hostages at four days before the inauguration of his successor, it was foreseeable that agreement would appear possible when the deadline came but would only actually occur on Inauguration Day, the real deadline.

Internal or external, any deadline has two dimensions— reasonableness and seriousness. A deadline that does not leave enough time for negotiation will either not be respected or will produce only a symbolic agreement (depending on its second dimension, seriousness, discussed below). If the overly tight deadline cannot be waived, the agreement may come on time, to avoid sanctions, but it will only confirm points already agreed on or provide a vague declaration of intentions that does not solve the basic issues. Such an agreement is an admission that deadline tactics—or perhaps simply the pressure of time—have been used too rigidly, leading the parties to think most about the stigma and setback of breakdown. Some critics, such as Garthoff

(1977, p. 39), look at SALT I in this light, disagreeing with Newhouse's previously cited evaluation. Deadline after deadline was passed in the Law of the Sea talks since 1976, simply because the parties needed the time to establish their own interests and the technical facts of the problem, before being able to work through the formula and the details of an agreement. Whatever the problems the United States had with President Thieu, there were simply not enough points of detail covered in the U.S.–Vietnamese agreements by the deadline mandated by the U.S. elections (which left only a month between the time of the North Vietnamese acceptance of the U.S. proposal and the time when the agreement was expected). Unresolved points included details both of the settlement itself and of the machinery for resolving future problems that were bound to arise.

The other dimension is seriousness. Although the point should be obvious in the definition it is often missed in practice: a deadline is only as strong as the sanctions behind it. If a deadline has serious consequences already written into it, parties should make this clear to each other, and if not, it is in their interest to put some teeth into the deadline at the beginning, before they get to the point where they need its effects. Such sanctions must be equal, although not identical, and their effects must be felt by both sides, at least in proportion to their original propensity to come to an agreement. The Namibian negotiations provide a sorry example of the inability of the parties to hold to a deadline, in this case because the Western mediators were unwilling to apply sanctions in September 1978 on South Africa and unable to conceive of graduated sanctions they might be willing to apply. In November 1958 and June 1961, Khrushchev imposed six-month deadlines for the solution of the status of Berlin, but he lacked the power to make his deadlines stick and lifted them after they had passed (Whelan 1979, pp. 284–85). The May 16, 1980, deadline for the

Palestine autonomy talks also lacked sanctions and so was ignored. The Cuban missile crisis of 1962 stands in contrast as a dramatic case of deadline bargaining. Attorney General Robert Kennedy's diary (1969, pp. 13, 14, 86, 87) is heavy with references to the pressure of the day (October 28) when the missiles would become operational and the United States would attack:

> Time was slowly running out. . . . Our military experts advised that these missiles could be in operation within a week. . . . Then it would be too late to do anything in Cuba, for by that time all their missiles would be operational. . . . [27 October] We had to have a commitment by tomorrow that those bases would be removed. I was not giving them an ultimatum but a statement of fact. [Dobrynin] should understand that if they did not remove those bases, we would remove them. . . . Time was running out. We had only a few more hours.

In those hours, the agreement was reached.

Deadlines tend to facilitate agreement, lower expectations, call bluffs, and produce final proposals, but also lead negotiators to adopt a tough position that will make them look good if—and therefore when—negotiations fail. They often have a sort of "musical chairs" effect (since musical chairs is a game that hangs on surprise deadlines): Parties tend to come to an agreement wherever they are when the deadline hits, but, this being the case, they try to maneuver to be in the best position when the music stops, whether there is an agreement or not. The effect that deadlines have on bargaining behavior and concession rates is therefore contradictory in experiment as well as in practice (Bartos 1974). Deadlines often force parties to come together, but sometimes the parties soften and sometimes they harden their positions. The clearest pattern seems to be a combination of the two: as a deadline approaches, parties harden their positions, spar and feint, in preparation for a last minute jump that will present the other with an offer that will be barely acceptable but too late to improve on. Relieved—or so the scenario goes—the other party does one of two things. He agrees, rationalizing that it is "the best he can do" and that there is "no time left to make any real improvements." He conjectures that with the deadline at hand, were he to refuse he would have to bear the opprobrium of breaking off negotiations; if he accepts, justification can be found in the fact that the deadline made this the last opportunity for an agreement. Or else he continues to withhold his agreement, letting the first party bargain "with himself" to improve the details of his proposal, agreeing at the very end of the last minute with minor rectifications that bring the advantages of the first party's "jump" to the other party's side.

The United States and the Soviet Union were under time pressure to have a draft treaty on nonproliferation to head off a U.N. initiative for a conference in the absence of any movement from them—an external deadline. The American negotiator recounted his decision to wait as long as possible before putting his last offer on the table—enough time to get confirmation from the Soviets, but not enough time for them to counter. He wanted to avoid the situation of putting forward a last offer and then seeing that offer "nickeled and dimed" by the other side's requests for several last concessions. "That is why there is so much hedging. Each side is trying to have the final word on the other party's final offer" (Fisher interview).

Later, the deadline with its pressures and dangers was present in the hectic final session of SALT. "Negotiating against a deadline is always risky. But by arranging to sign a SALT agreement in Moscow, that is what Nixon elected to do. In effect, he placed himself in what French diplomats call the worst of positions: *demandeur*. It is hard for the other side to react to a self-appointed *demandeur* other than to exploit him. Yet, as it turned out, nobody seems to have been exploited. Brezhnev wanted, and apparently felt he needed, the agreements as much as Nixon" (Newhouse 1973, p. 270).

When a basic phenomenon and its effects are as well established as is the deadline scenario, alternatives grow up, sometimes to the point of crowding out the original phenomenon. Three variants have evolved in response to deadlines. One alternative is to stop the clock. Clocks can be stopped literally, as in legislative sessions, or figuratively, by simply extending the sessions and pushing the implicit deadline back. The Egyptians and Israelis had until twelve o'clock to wrap up their negotiations and the clock was stopped to do so. (First the concept of clock-stopping had to be explained to both parties!) An agreement officially signed on one day was actually signed a day later. When the clock is literally stopped there is a real but implicit deadline working, and that is how long the legislators can stay awake. In other cases the new deadline is less evident, and something may have to be done to restore limits or make a deadline. In the Golan Heights disengagement talks in 1974, Kissinger used the threat of leaving as a deadline, renewable on occasion, and in talks on the second Sinai disengagement in 1975 he actually had to implement one such threat to make the next deadline credible. A new deadline can be agreed upon, a new threat of sanctions made. A sense of impending troubles or of fraying tempers can also weigh on the negotiators, gradually imposing time costs. The limited time available for the Camp David meeting between Presidents Carter and Sadat and Prime Minister Begin in 1978 and for Carter's Middle East trip in 1979 carried its own deadlines that were effective in producing agreement. A series of stepped sanctions can be imposed, worsening conditions by successive time periods. Or, a "reverse deadline" can be imposed, implementing a threat and promising its removal instead of

threatening a sanction at a certain date. The Arab oil embargo provided a reverse deadline for the Middle East disengagements in 1974, and was lifted when they were signed,
and the Syrian mini-war of attrition early in the same year
reinforced the same deadline. The Christmas bombing of
Vietnam was a reverse deadline in part, with the United
States bombing until the North Vietnamese agreed to return
to the table, since the deadline date implied by the American
elections had passed without an agreement (Zartman 1976,
pp. 390–91, 396–97). The reverse deadline can also be imposed sporadically, to reinforce the reality of the sanctions
so that they may not be needed at the end.

Unfortunately, the response to deadline situations must
also be taken into account. A "self-proving hypothesis"
reaction may occur, as parties facing a deadline and
toughening behavior on the part of the opponent start preparing their minds for failure and looking for ways to explain it. The opponent becomes the scapegoat and the party
begins to act in a way that forces the opponent to play out his
role. Instead of preparing to come to an agreement at the last
minute, they begin to prepare to disagree. Sometimes this is
the best position from which to force the other party to make
the final concession, but sometimes preparations for failure
are too far along to permit acceptance of the final concession
when at last it comes. In 1956, the United States and the
United Nations were gradually nearing success in bringing
together the positions of Egypt on one side and Britain and
France on the other in the Suez crisis. But in the end Britain
and France were simply too far gone in their commitment to
a unilateral solution to be able to recognize the acceptability
of Egyptian concessions, and the war began. The same momentum can affect the domestic support for the negotiators, as in the example below.

The single biggest problem with SALT was delay. The

negotiations had dragged on for too long. The saga of SALT II had become a shaggy dog story of anticlimaxes and missed deadlines. To mention just one, the expiration of the SALT I interim agreement on offensive weapons had occurred two years before, in October 1977; the deadline had been extended artificially, by an exchange of "unilateral" statements of open-ended intent to continue adhering to the SALT I limits. But American domestic support for a new treaty lost much of its momentum, while opposition gained steadily, in a political climate of growing anger, fear and frustration directed at the Soviet Union. (Talbot 1980, p. 529)

This is the final paradox of the negotiating process. Negotiators need a deadline in most cases, or else the search for agreeable details resembles an academic study group. Yet deadlines and the behavior associated with them often press them to prepare for the worst.

BEHAVIOR IN THE DETAIL PHASE: A SUMMARY

The detail phase consists of a long, tense search for agreement on details to implement the general framework set out in the previous phase. In reality, the two are not as separate as this phraseology might imply, but they do contain different elements and outcomes. As parties announce positions on details, they can either exchange agreements on different points or they can concede their way to some point in between their initial positions. Wherever possible, it is better to group, package, or exchange concessions rather than to fight it out over separate issues taken individually, since the former allows for greater total payoffs and greater possibility for satisfaction for each side on at least some of the points, and therefore facilitates agreement. Yet sometimes big issues must be handled individually. Usually the number of details agreed upon increases as the end of negotiations approaches, and the existence of a specific deadline generally causes parties to hold out until they are ready to establish final positions just before the time runs out.

Every approach to the regulation of details has its dangers. Mutual concessions tend to leave no one happy and may result in agreement on a very artificial point (like the 38th Parallel in Korea). Concessions may be misinterpreted, cooperativeness may be mistaken for weakness, and innovativeness may engender suspicion. Exchanges of agreements may also set up contradictions and may not settle the points where denial is as much a part of a party's stand as acquisition. Tactical holdout for deadlines may leave too little time for constructive agreement, and the deadline may come and go without agreement on enough points to make for a comprehensive solution. Deadlines may distort or interrupt the natural convergence of views developing in the negotiating process.

More than any other phase, the arrangement of details is marked by contradictions and paradoxes. The "first level effect" of many of its mechanisms is well enough known that parties are able to plan appropriate counterstrategies, and the problem of infinite regress engulfs careful planning. The "toughness–softness" cycle seems to defy advice, and "mixed strategy" may appear as a synonym for no strategy at all. Yet in the end there may be less room for debate in retrospect over detailed agreements than over the formula that preceded them, other than the debate over completeness. The broadest and most unbridgeable debate in the Cuban missile crisis or in the Paris negotiations over Vietnam is still not about details but about competing or potential formulas, and the same thing is true to a lesser extent over SALT and to a much greater extent about Mideast peace negotiations.

Yet the nature of the search for agreement on details means that the seekers should keep a special checklist on their desks, to avoid some inherent pitfalls that are not otherwise signaled in the process.

1. *Do not lose the big picture in the little picture.*

Negotiations on details—sometimes left to subordinates—lead the negotiators to focus on smaller and smaller items, away from the broad framework. It is possible, as seen, to undo the formula with its details, either by inattention or by design. It is also possible to put together a sloppy and incoherent agreement where the little pieces simply do not fit together to make a whole out of the parts. Several of the other items on the checklist are more specific extensions of this theme.

2. *Be clear from the beginning about objectives, and do not confuse means with ends.*

Innovation, flexibility, and the ability to seize opportunities are one thing, but uncertainty about priorities and goals is another. The line is thin, of course, and often parties have to settle for less than they originally wanted, but they should not shift their sights among a range of equally obtainable goals. Even Kissinger had to cover the American shifts in priorities in SALT with a quip, but the uncertainties have given rise to some sound reflections by his advisors (Garthoff 1977, pp. 22, 23): "Negotiating objectives must be clear and consistent. Bargaining room and bargaining chips have a place, but as means and not as part of the objective; it is necessary to keep leeway for compromise without constant reshuffle of goals." And again, making a helpful, if schematic, distinction between leeway in formula and in details: "Calculated ambiguity on 'quantities' (literally and figuratively) may be useful, but not on essential qualities of the objective."

3. *Steadiness on the brink requires a clear understanding of increments and a sense of both sides' ability to do without an agreement.*

Negotiation of details is the time for deadline bargaining and calculations of toughness. However much one might try to conceive of negotiation as the peaceful settlement of disputes or the friendly reconciliation of differences, there is always an eyeball-to-eyeball moment when parties must weigh holding out against nonagreement. Sometimes this is overdone, sometimes not done enough when the stakes warrant it. Sometimes it is done unconvincingly, without full awareness of the balance sheet, or for the wrong audience over the wrong details. Finding the correct answer to questions of "when" and "how" to concede can be aided by taking account of the points made in the preceding discussion, even if in part it is a matter of personality, skill, and experience.

4. *Concessions are made to convey a message but they are justified by principle.*

The way in which a party concedes, in time, in increments, and in degree, carries messages to the other party. But the winning argument to clinch a decision on a detail at X rather than at Y depends on conveying a sense of principle and of value, and also of coherence within the ensemble of the emerging agreement. Questions the negotiator must ask himself are: Is the justification valid? Does the other party need the item in order to make the agreement stick, and need it more than I do? Can I afford to let him have it? Does it fit the overall concept or formula of the agreement? The best argument is therefore the one that answers these questions best.

6

Structuring Negotiations

Negotiation takes place not only between conflicting views of salient issues; it also involves conflict among parties. Even if there is a stalemate in the attainment of goals, this does not mean that the parties are basically equal or even similar. The previous discussion has treated negotiation as a symmetrical process in which tactics and strategies available to one party are also available to the other, making it impossible to provide theoretical advice on how to win. Yet the preceding chapters have also noted from time to time that the parties may be in very different positions in relation to each other and to the central issue. There are have-nots wanting to buy into the haves without standard currency; there are *demandeurs* seeking to equalize status or possession from an initial position of inequality; there are losers trying to cut their losses and winners looking for half a victory at lower cost; there are revolutionaries trying to break the old order and defenders of that order trying to buy off revolutionaries whom they cannot defeat. Furthermore, although it was maintained from the beginning that negotiation is different, as a process, from coalition and therefore that the "weight" of the parties does not count as votes, there is no pure process in reality and teams do "weigh in" differently. There are newcomers who are oversensitive when confronted with established parties; there are parties dominated by their national administration or by their chief, facing others that are loose collections of competing authorities; there are teams with their own authority and others who are merely messengers. Much can be learned about the negotiating process under the assumptions of symmetry, but now it is time to relax that assumption and examine the opportunities open to negotiators when the parties are unsymmetrical.

THE WEIGHT OF THE SIDES

One of the eternal paradoxes of negotiation is that it allows the weak to confront the strong and still come away with something which should not be possible if weakness and strength were all that mattered. Much depends on definition, so that terms such as "weak" and "strong" have come to be used sloppily and inappropriately in discussions of negotiation. Nonetheless, there is usually a general appreciation of the power position of parties—so that Europe facing Africa, or Britain facing Malta, or the North facing the South can be seen as cases where the strong negotiated with the weak, respectively. Of course, even such gross evaluations must be tempered by other considerations, such as the shifting fortunes of the moment. The oil companies will be seen as the strong when facing the oil countries prior to 1970, then the tables turned so that OPEC was the stronger in the decade of the October war; and by the end of the decade the United States had returned to a position of considerable power vis-à-vis OPEC, even though a consumer country.

Technology does not yet permit measuring the power imbalance between negotiating parties, but it can be recognized enough to allow drawing conclusions about differences in behavior. At least one can be forewarned, knowing what to expect from a stronger or weaker opponent; at best one might be forearmed as well, knowing how to counter the tactic.

Weaker parties tend to seek more formal negotiating forums and to strengthen their hand through organization.

"Organization," wrote Michels (p. 61) in his famous dictum, "is the weapon of the weak in their struggle with the strong." An earlier study on the negotiating tactics of the weak versus the strong (Zartman 1971, pp. 227–28) concluded that the power of the weaker states was a procedural power that lay in the ability to choose and exploit their terrain. "Weak states can provoke an encounter . . . they can put forward their needs. . . . Weak states have the power to agree." These tactics are maximized in organized negotiating forums. Similarly, the tendency of the weaker parties to seek strength in unity leads to the conclusion to be discussed further below, that group decisions have the disadvantage of slowness but the advantage of rigidity. A group becomes its own public, increasing the commitment of its spokesmen and reducing their flexibility.

Weak states can afford erratic or irresponsible behavior more easily than stronger parties, particularly when the rules of regularity and responsibility favor the strong.

Schelling has spoken of coercive deficiency as a persuasive tactic of the weak, who cry for help lest they do something that everyone will regret. It has already been noted that *demandeurs* often begin high and wild and then concede rapidly, if only to strengthen the notion of moral obligation that favors them. Weak parties can also escalate demands rather than making concessions, in a tactic that would be seen as bullying and nonnegotiatory if practiced by the strong. In fact, it is usually in weak parties' interests not to make concessions at all until they have been convinced of the good faith of a stronger party through initial concessions.

Weak states do best by rewarding stronger states' concessions rather than by "hanging tough" and by opening high to indicate needs and to facilitate rewards.

The tactics of toughness and softness vary according to the strength of the parties; under symmetry, toughness tends to lead to toughness and under asymmetry to softness, with weaker parties following the lead of stronger parties (Pruitt 1981, pp. 1, 18, 25).

THE SIZE OF THE TEAM

Each side in a negotiation is expected to speak with one voice, and yet a delegation usually has more than one member. Before diplomacy became a bureaucratic function the negotiator was often on his own, attended at most by a personal aide. Today, negotiating teams can—and often must—be enormous because of the technical complexity of the issues, although real movement still is often accomplished by a few chief negotiators meeting together. At the Geneva Conference on the Middle East, in late 1973, Foreign Ministers Gromyko and Eban were in a room with three Russian and three Israeli aides when Gromyko said, "Look, something strange is occurring. Sitting here are six men who are thinking the same thing: 'How can we leave our two ministers so they can speak alone?'" The six aides got the hint and left, although no settlement emerged as a result (Golan 1976, p. 139). During the Trieste negotiations, the real bargaining began when teams were dismissed and the American and the British representatives negotiated first with the Yugoslav emissary and then with the Italian. But these instances have become more the exception than the rule and in nearly all negotiations today a delegation is plural. What are the implications of this situation? How many people should be on the negotiating team itself? What happens to those who are left behind? How are information, instructions, and decisions to be handled among them?

Group decisions are hard to undo.

They are really not a different order of things but rather a further extension of the negotiation process. If decisions are made solely by one authority, by the delegation leader or the chief back home, they fall under a different decision-making process. But usually they involve a good deal of intragroup, interagency, home-to-mission, actor-to-audience negotiation. Decisions arrived at in this way are obviously complicated and often time-consuming, and they have given rise among scholars to models of negotiation as a collection of bureaucratic positions presumably held together by the necessity of finding a way to say something to the opponent. In this, the more frequent situation, the authority of the delegation leader depends on his skill as an aggregator who makes a balanced whole out of the parts' sum.

The picture is true, if incomplete, and seems to be a universal characteristic of complex modern organizations, whether the American or the Soviet government or the European Community or OPEC. J. Robert Schaetzel, who represented the United States at the European Community, commented on the great importance of negotiation within the delegation: "In a democracy such as this engaged in international negotiations, about 90 percent of the problem is the negotiation with one's compatriots, and getting the other agencies largely to agree to a common position. Dealing with foreigners tends to be a day in the country in comparison with that" (Schaetzel interview). A single important case study found the same trait on both sides: "Finally, and importantly, SALT is an internal negotiation. It is within the two capitals that the critical bargaining—the struggle to grind out a position—lumbers endlessly, episodically on" (Newhouse 1973, p. 32). This explains the long delays in arriving at a group position, and since the phenomenon is universally recognized it is the basis for a powerful negotiating argument directed toward the other side: Take it or leave it but don't rock the boat. A prominent American statesman once told the Europeans that by the time the United States government was ready to negotiate a position it was often so firmly fixed because of internal negotiations and agreements that it had little give. Therefore, if the Europeans wished to have an impact on the U.S. position, he urged, they must find ways of introducing their ideas before the United States had reached a formal position. The European Communities in turn have used their own divisions and difficulties in arriving at a decision to the same effect, the "friendly" European state urging a third party to accept an EEC compromise lest an "unfriendly" state prevail if the compromise is rejected.

The size and complexity of the delegation can therefore be used as the rationale for a warning ("You had better accept this package that we put together with such difficulty, because if you don't we will never be able to get together on another one"). In much the same way one of the several members can be cast in the role of the "heavy," to justify the warning in another form ("You had better accept this package because if you don't, we moderates will lose control of the delegation and my colleague here will become the spokesman"). One might think that statesmen would be beyond the "good cop–bad cop" routine, and yet it has been used effectively on occasion. President Sadat put his foreign minister, Ismail Fahmy, and his chief of staff, General Mohammed Gamasy, in the heavy role in front of Kissinger. Then when they left the room, Sadat could show how sweet and reasonable he was, thus giving force to the point, a moment later, when he dug in his heels on another matter (Golan 1976, p. 160). President Nixon and Secretary Kissinger played their roles together.

> In negotiating technique, Nixon and Kissinger put on a formidable display, like a two-man interrogation team where one man holds a truncheon and the other offers a cigarette. Nixon's way was to appear rigid, sit tight for a long time, and then go for a "bold new approach" that can be considerably different from his original position. Kissinger, to the contrary, was willing to invest heavily . . . to achieve bargaining credibility, that is, an understanding by his adversary that a Kissinger proposal has about five degrees of leeway in it and no more. . . . There was an added complexity: sometimes Kissinger played the tough guy, sometimes Nixon did. (Safire 1975, pp. 442 ff.)

But the size and complexity of a delegation is not an unmixed advantage. If a pluralistic delegation can be played off against itself by its spokesman, it can also be played upon by the opponent. The theoretical discussion of this possibility usually involves the concept of coalition, which may be going a bit far in most negotiations. The Russians are not going to coopt a member of the American SALT team, nor even will the Israelis and Arabs or Europeans and Africans form coalitions that cut across the "sides" in their negotiations. But lesser variations on "coalition" are eminently possible, ranging anywhere from attempts to widen natural rifts within the opponent, to taking members of the other team aside to explain things in terms to which they are individually receptive. A comment on SALT provides an insight applicable to many negotiations: "To my knowledge, there were no instances on either side of disloyalty to a delegation or its instructed position. But there were issues on which some delegates and advisers sought earnestly to persuade members of the other delegation, which their compatriots did not" (Garthoff 1977a, p. 79).

Moreover, as previously mentioned, if an individual has been involved in a continuing negotiation over a long period of time, he may come to think of his primary interest as getting some movement in the negotiation. During SALT such situations arose on both sides. "In a broad sense, they were becoming accomplices, seeking to narrow differences between their governments, looking for bargaining room. This other tendency indicated, among other things, that SALT had slid into deep trouble" (Newhouse 1973, p. 212). Yet when the time of troubles was over, Russians and Americans paired off after hours during the SALT talks to get their messages across better than they could in plenary session. Similarly, in the European–African negotiations on association agreements, the French and the French-speaking Africans became each other's spokesmen, not at the cost of their own interests but frequently viewing their own interests in such a way as to be compatible with their role as spokesman for the other party. It is to guard against this type of divisive influence that delegates from authoritarian or ideological states travel in pairs or not at all.

Another reason for pluralistic delegations to establish among themselves some authority for decision-making is that *the larger the number of equal parties involved on a side the more difficult it is to arrive at a position.* The arithmetic of the process is proof enough: the number of possible fences to keep mended, relations to tend, and interests to protect rises geometrically with a simple increase in the number of parties. Moreover, different authorities and audiences back home have to be satisfied, with a second-level problem of fences, relations, and interests. When, in a multistate negotiation, all parties are legally equal, coalitions in a real sense are established. Then decisions can be reached only by intraparty negotiations, and all the previous discussion in this book applies.

Various agencies of government may share the same view on the overall framework of a negotiation, yet vary on the strategy that should be pursued. In the midst of the Sixth Special Session of the U.N. General Assembly, both the State and the Treasury Departments saw the negotiations in terms of "them versus us," yet took different positions on the strategy the United States should pursue. While State tended to favor actions that would provide diplomatic flexibility, Treasury took the harder line that mistaken concessions at that time would lead to gross difficulties later on. When the Americans were negotiating with Algeria on the El Paso natural gas deal, they had to be careful in their choice of Algerian ministries to deal with, to avoid being caught in disputes between the Energy and Foreign Ministries.

Since the approval of various government agencies will be required to conclude agreements, it is useful to have people in the delegation who have the direct confidence of the top man in their particular department. Such team members may be useful in advising what such an agency of government can live with and then, once they are convinced of what is needed, in exerting their influence to persuade members of their department.

Averell Harriman drew on two negotiations from his own experience to illustrate the importance of having key people from various departments on a delegation: "In the so-called Anglo-American mission, I had a group of very competent men with me who were very helpful in advising me and in persuading the different agencies, the Army, the Navy, Air Force, and Lend-Lease, to supply materials and so forth. Once they were sold on what was needed, they were most valuable in using their influence" (Harriman interview).

In the nuclear test-ban negotiations I had a well-balanced group. We had a first-class fellow from the Pentagon, John McNaughton. He had the confidence of McNamara. I also had Butch Fisher, who had worked with me in

Commerce. He was second to Bill Foster in the arms control field. We had Bill Tyler, Assistant Secretary of State for Europe. He didn't really have to play much of a role except to keep the State Department fully informed. We had scientists. And then I got Carl Kaysen to come from the White House. You want to have somebody in the group who has a pipeline to the top in each place. (Harriman interview)

The need to win approval at home is crucial if the negotiations are to be successful. Particular difficulties are imposed by the American system in which all treaties require Senate ratification and an executive agreement requires a majority of both Houses or at least the absence of opposition. But these are merely more formal instances of the same problems that the president–dictator of Panama has in keeping his support once the canal issue is solved more or less on his terms, or that the Soviet party chief has in maneuvering a Cuban missile solution or a SALT formula and details through the Politburo while still retaining his post. Furthermore, the American president is certain not to lose his job in the process, whereas Torrijos and Khrushchev and Brezhnev might. Furthermore, contrary to common images, both President Sadat and Prime Minister Begin are subject to interest group negotiations and "audience" controls, the latter operating under threat of a revolt in parliament and the former under threat of revolt in the street.

John Hickerson was part of the team that negotiated the NATO treaty. Throughout the negotiations, he recalled, the Senate Foreign Relations Committee was kept abreast of developments:

We went up once or twice a week, and the Senate Foreign Relations Committee knew every word in the treaty. They made suggestions, and if they were at all reasonable we tried to get—and in most cases got—them accepted.

There was no leak in the Senate. I mean this was off the record, but at the time negotiations were completed we issued the text before the treaty was signed. Practically every member of the Foreign Relations Committee had a vested interest in that treaty and contributed to it. Of course we got an overwhelming vote of approval. (Hickerson interview)

There is one other set of tactics that can be used when there are many partners on one side, known in some circles as leapfrogging or shooting pigeons. Faced with a "side" that is at best a confederation of many countries with separate but sometimes converging interests, Libyans and labor unions alike have found it convenient to concentrate on the most vulnerable members of the confederation, negotiate in terms of that member's interests, and then move on down the line, knocking off the other members one by one. This was the approach that the Israeli government hoped that Sadat was suggesting when he went to Jerusalem in the name of the Arabs. Under the best of conditions, negotiators can then return to the first party and rectify any omissions in the light of agreements negotiated with the last. Against this process of singleshooting and leapfrogging, the other parties can impose unity rules and tighten their confederation, as OPEC and the Arab states did, and as the oil companies had previously done. The tactic of driving a wedge between opponents is not as scurrilous or unusual as some comments might suggest. It is similar to the more frequent tactic of dividing the issues and signing an agreement on the elements that parties can agree on, while isolating the issues on which they cannot agree.

In sum, the pluralism of delegations can contribute to either flexibility or rigidity in national positions. A delegation with a number of components can use them for flexibility but is also vulnerable to their being used to the same end by the other party. When such a delegation reaches an agreement, it has the strengths and weaknesses of rigidity—being stuck with positions that are in danger of being unacceptable to the other side. It is for this reason that delegations usually develop a degree of authority and hierarchy, even if they are multinational delegations that did not start with these qualities, for someone must decide on the limits of flexibility and rigidity (Rubin and Brown 1975, p. 51). The Africans were all flexibility in the Yaounde negotiations with the European Communities in 1962 and 1967 and they undercut each other on occasion; they developed a proper amount of trust and discipline by the time of the Lomé negotiations. Without some hierarchy, the three Zimbabwe delegations in Geneva in 1976 were just about impossible to negotiate with, since each was ready to undercut the others. The only antidote considered was to add several other Rhodesian delegations alongside Smith, but this was hard to implement. As a result, those delegations with a sense of hierarchy among them struck out on their own and negotiated an agreement with Smith and Salisbury.

Even when there is clear hierarchy and authority, problems may remain. One is illustrated in Averell Harriman's views on the most effective size for a delegation:

> The group should be very small and very carefully picked. I think the smaller the staff the lighter the head man's burden. I cut the staff down very much in the Laos negotiations. Before the staff was cut I was working hours and hours conferring with staff members. But when I cut the staff, I discovered that I had plenty of time for myself. When there was a big staff there were a lot of people who weren't fully occupied, and they'd want to charge in and see me and tell me all about their complaints about not being consulted about this or that. So I had to have staff

meetings. When I had a small staff everybody was overworked; we had a minimum of staff meetings, and they bothered me very little. I've become a great convert to Parkinson's Law since I've come back to government. The important thing is to give each person something to do, or have a subcommittee of two or three to work on getting papers together. If you don't, they're going to be troublesome.

The psychology of negotiations is important, particularly when you're in a tough place like Moscow where you feel rather restricted. The morale of the team is extremely important, and the chairman of the group has to be a fellow who can pull people together. (Harriman interview)

THE FOLKS BACK HOME

Nobody suggests that negotiating teams should include the entire public, yet the public must be taken into account. Even those of an older school who still prefer secret covenants secretly negotiated must admit that some day, when the covenant becomes operative, the public will find out. Where, along the spectrum of possibilities, the proper relationship between responsible official and informed public lies is a question of major importance. The arguments are simple enough and well known. "Too great" publicity for the negotiations is inefficient, for it draws negotiators to the windows to address the public rather than each other, and makes for inflexible positions. Negotiators become locked in by their public's expectations. Behind-the-scenes compromises become more difficult. Theodore Kheel, who has witnessed many labor negotiations, commented on how negotiators become prisoners of their public positions:

Top leadership has a constituency—take the Ocean Hill dispute [in the New York city public school system] where you had a lot of people who were new to negotiations, with an uncertain constituency, in fact a constituency for which they were competing with other leaders. The Reverend Oliver, Rhody McCoy and [Albert] Shanker would have to take public positions like "We will never give up on this" that made it very difficult for them later on to give up on it. They put their feet in cement. . . . A good negotiator knows how to keep his constituency behind him without taking positions that become impossible for him to change. (Kheel interview)

The Trieste negotiations of 1954 were carried on in almost total secrecy. The U.S. negotiator, Llewellyn Thompson, was at the time high commissioner in Austria and gave out the story that he was in London to buy clothes (foreshadowing Kissinger's famous "covers" during the Vietnam, Russian, and Chinese negotiations). His conclusion was that "the main lesson is the necessity of negotiating in secret on things of this sort, particularly anything that involves territory, because the moment a government takes a public position on a territorial issue, a retreat is almost impossible" (Campbell 1976, p. 40).

Yet, "too little" publicity is considered undemocratic, may lead to shady deals, and in the end is probably inefficient too, since at some point in the process of ratification the press and other media will comment on the agreement and bring it under public scrutiny. It is therefore easier in a democratic country to sell an agreement to an audience that understands the process of putting it together and the value of the agreement. Without such understanding, the president may have to undertake a broad campaign to promote acceptance of an agreement. President Carter himself went experience, that an appeal from the president of the United States was the instrumental difference in reaching agreement on stabilizing the price of a commodity:

> I approached the talks [with Eduardo Frei, president of Chile] by explaining the difficulties our president had in the world, and his concern for maintaining the stability of the United States and avoiding inflation. But the important thing about this was that I simply said to him, "The President of the United States has sent me to see you and ask your help." He said, "You make it very difficult for me. There's nothing that is more difficult for me to do." The next day he asked me to come back. He said he had thought over our discussion and would accept a substantial compromise. This is a very important thing, to know when you can appeal to a man's better instincts. It was sobering for him to think that he, the president of rather a small country, had received such a request. (Harriman interview)

It may also be discouraging to the delegation not to be informed of higher level initiatives, but secrecy is sometimes necessary to break impasses. Front channels are also useful for totally different functions, notably as a public negotiating screen for more delicate private talks. The front channel may be the propaganda arm, covering up for concessions, or it may be the intelligence arm, sounding out the other side on its demands and flexibility in preparation for a direct offer through the back channel. A problem can arise, of course, when the front channel thinks it is negotiating rather than merely emitting propaganda or receiving intelligence.

Good examples of different uses of front and back channels are found in the SALT I and the Paris Vietnam negotiations. In the former, much work was done by the front channel, both in negotiation and intelligence, but the back was needed on occasion to break up logjams. In the latter, little

on television to "sell" the Panama Canal agreement and also sent members of his administration across the nation to do the same.

To try to find one's way through this debate, one must admit that the argument in favor of secrecy in negotiation is right, even if that does not make the argument in favor of informing the public wrong. Many kinds of rewards and much expert knowledge are at the disposal of the press and the public, and negotiators—particularly when they are politicians—can be expected to be sensitive to them. The public image of negotiation as concession clashes with citizens' views of their leaders and representatives as strong for the right, courageous against odds, unshakable under fire, and not prone to cave in, sell out, give up, or be walked over. Public and press can enmesh a negotiator in a net of symbols, loyalties, obligations, and accountability procedures that keep his latitude limited. It is enough to drive any conscientious negotiator to secrecy.

Negotiators may themselves make statements to assuage or divert public opinion, as Harriman explained: "Now, there are plenty of things that we have to say for our domestic record, and it's always well to tell the other fellow, 'Don't pay too much attention to that, we have to say these things. You know they're not true, I'm saying them not for your benefit but for the home public. You know them already'" (Harriman interview). In fact, a major problem for a negotiator is to separate the noise from the message, a problem far more difficult and more complex than such a simple statement might suggest. Thus because the external context is heavy with noise, negotiators seek secrecy where they can concentrate on the message.

In an age of mass communications, a new and complicating factor in negotiations is that negotiators may seek to influence public opinion in other countries than their own. Many observers commented on President Sadat's skillful use of the mass media to publicize his positions in his negotiations with Israel in late 1977 and to reach out to audiences in the United States, the Middle East, and around the world; over the next three years one of his strategies was to educate the Israeli population to put pressure on its leaders from below, and he eventually helped defeat the Begin government at the polls. The mass media have become a tool of negotiations: a way of mobilizing support, of bringing pressure to bear that goes beyond those few people who have decision-making power, and also a way of limiting and shaping the options open to decision-makers (see Lewis, 1977).

The arguments against secrecy are no less correct. Secrecy is no refuge, since at some point the public will know anyhow. In an age of so-called sunshine laws, it may even have a right to know early in the process. Controlled information from a high government source may meet the requirements, but the major underlying argument about accountable and responsible government returns: as long as there is no way to verify what officials say, we cannot know whether the information is correct, so why should high officials play it straight?

In the end, what is important is the balance between the attainment of concrete results and the retention of abstract values. The fact is that there are few examples of a publicly negotiated solution of a difficult conflict. Even where open sessions are held—as in the United Nations—the real negotiations take place in the corridors or behind closed doors. Another fact is that delaying public disclosure of the process merely postpones the debate, often to a less favorable time. The delay in no way guarantees or even facilitates ratification. But the countervailing fact is that secrecy too often leads to abuse. Somewhere between "too much" and "too little" is an optimal working compromise, involving se-

cret negotiations, participation of public re and regular news accounts whenever possible

HIGHER AND LOWER AND FRONT AND BACK CHANNELS

The relationship between the negotiator a front may be described in terms of channels. channel can be most useful if it is not used to e undercut or replace the negotiator's role at t table. This study does not seek to deal compreh the subject of summitry, that is, formal pro cussions between heads of state, a subject t much discussed elsewhere. Suffice it to say l ventional summitry is looked upon with cons ticism by most practicing negotiators because cannot be adequately familiar with all of th complex negotiation. Summits, however, can t formalizing agreements previously hammere gotiating teams; and (2) in developing persona between heads of state that may be utilized at in future negotiations. These relationships m to as back channels. If things get stuck up fron takes the prestige and flexibility of a high lev an inside track to the head of state or gover things moving again or to float a new approac lost in the front channel. It is not always fl working delegation up front, but sometimes it restore momentum.

The letter from President Eisenhower tha phy carried in 1954 to President Tito of Yugo ing for his help in getting the logjam broken dispute is credited by Vladimir Velebit, the gotiator, with reopening communication (C p. 103). Harriman also relates, in another inc work was done at the official negotiating sessions but they provided a screen of verbiage that the Vietnamese seemed to find useful and that, again, enabled each side to probe the other side's intentions. Sometimes one wonders whether such elaborate—and, after all, expensive—charades are necessary. The answer may well lie in requirements of the respective cultures; even the three years of Vietnam negotiations, with all their misunderstanding and hostility, seemed to require a semipublic forum as well as a secret substance in order to make progress. Something, no matter how hostile and outwardly unproductive, was necessary to symbolize continuity when the secret talks were on the rocks.

LONG AND SHORT REINS

The subject of diplomatic reins, also concerns the relationship between the head of state and the negotiator. Few diplomats—or at least few Western diplomats—like to be merely mouthpieces, unable to agree even on the next meeting date without a word from the home office. But there are occasions when the chief executive wants to hold a negotiator on a short rein. Averell Harriman recounted such an instance from his experience:

> During the war, I think one of the reasons why Roosevelt picked me was because he knew that I wouldn't give him any trouble. If he'd picked a member of his cabinet, it might be different. For instance, when I went to negotiate the supply agreement in 1941, both Morgenthau and Knox were anxious to go, but he picked me. I think one of the reasons why he picked me was because he knew that he could overrule me and it wouldn't be of any embarrassment to him, whereas if he overruled a member of his Cabinet, it would be difficult. (Harriman interview)

On the other hand, few diplomats like to have total

latitude and responsibility without some indication of the limits of acceptability for an agreement that will ultimately have to be sold to the many jealous executive agencies, if not to a suspicious legislature.

A negotiator may take steps to insure access to the top decision-maker. In his memoirs, Dean Acheson wrote about his role as backstop to General George Marshall during his mission to China:

> The General said that he would need what was known in the Army as a rear echelon, a person left behind with right of access at any time to the Commander-in-Chief, in this case, the President, through whom General Marshall could communicate. This man would bear personal responsibility for immediate reply and for action upon his requests, with authority to call on the President himself for help, if necessary to get action. The General would want an Army officer detailed to handle incoming and outgoing messages through Army channels, which would be used exclusively, as they were the only reliable facilities in China. The officer would deliver the messages to the rear echelon personally. . . . General Marshall wanted personal, not institutional, responsibility. He was no stranger to Washington bureaucracy.
>
> When the President agreed and asked whom he would select, the General said that he would like to have me charged with this duty. He asked that my assuming it be cleared with Secretary Byrnes, pointing out that I would necessarily have to act out of channels and probably annoy a good many people in fulfilling this assignment. My intuition was entirely correct. (Acheson 1969, pp. 143–44)

Somewhere in between, perhaps closer to the pole of independent responsibility, is the most comfortable position for a negotiator. But there are two sides to each pole. A

negotiator finds it convenient to float personal ideas informally, perhaps even as a basis for making recommendations
back home. A negotiator also finds it useful to be able to hide
behind the need to get new instructions from time to time. In
other words, as might be expected, latitude is useful in putting forth one's own ideas and constraint is useful in accepting the other's proposals.

Negotiators often find it useful to be able to say that they
are limited in their ability to compromise or in their margin
of flexibility by instructions from home. "Checking back" is
a way to indicate a negotiator's flexibility on a given issue
without necessarily conceding a point. To say one is limited
by instructions or that one does not have the authority to
commit something may or may not be true, but it is a way to
test the waters for the temperature of the other side's position without necessarily making any commitments. Secretary Dulles at one time discussed a possible security treaty in
Australia with the Australians and New Zealanders. In the
end it looked as if a treaty would make sense, but Dulles left
behind a letter that said, "I must emphasize that I have not
authority to commit my Government to its acceptance. . . . As
I told you the instructions of our mission contemplated a
Pacific security arrangement more comprehensive than
merely a Treaty between three countries" (Spender 1969, p.
159).

Other means to maintain flexibility in negotiations are
measures that break the formal rigidity of plenary sessions,
such as the use of subordinates, corridors, and tea breaks.
Whether at the point of searching for a formula or hunting
down a detail, occasions to sound out "what would happen
if . . ." on an informal or personal basis are usually helpful.
In fact, one would think that a good negotiating team would
be continually bombarding the other party with ideas, variations, innovations, thrusting and sparring to try to find the
limits of acceptability, the points of real disagreement, the

holes in defense, the thickness of the arguments of the other side. The corollary is that each party should avoid debates and battles lest he force the other to dig in on an undesirable position. The point is to loosen up the other party, make him think in new ways, press him to face those points in his position that he can yield without compromising the essentials. As long as they do not lead to undermining one's own position on the essentials, any techniques of informal discussion are helpful.

THE CULTURAL CONTEXT OF NEGOTIATIONS

The most troublesome question at the end of an inquiry of this type concerns the role of culture. Do people from different cultures have a different conception of the function of negotiation? Do they negotiate differently? Immediately this simple question dissolves into a number of definitional difficulties and problems of generalization. Any question dealing with national cultures brings with it the pitfalls of stereotypes partly anchored in reality and partly imaginary. Do Arabs negotiate like rug merchants, Africans palaver, and Orientals negotiate inscrutably? But then, is the relevant family "Arab" or Saudi, Moroccan, Egyptian, and so forth? Do all Africans negotiate like "Africans?" Are all Orientals equally inscrutable? It is easy to show the ridiculous stereotypes on which cultural generalizations are based, and yet there is something under it all which conforms to reality.

Many analysts have considered the cultural context in writing about specific negotiations. Dennett and Johnson, for example, put together a useful collection on negotiating with the Russians, Whelan skillfully analyzed a quarter-century of experience since then, and Kennan added his own observations on their idiosyncrasies. One of the main pitfalls in wartime and immediate postwar Anglo–American negotiations with the Soviet Union, in Philip Mosely's view, on television to "sell" the Panama Canal agreement and also sent members of his administration across the nation to do the same.

To try to find one's way through this debate, one must admit that the argument in favor of secrecy in negotiation is right, even if that does not make the argument in favor of informing the public wrong. Many kinds of rewards and much expert knowledge are at the disposal of the press and the public, and negotiators—particularly when they are politicians—can be expected to be sensitive to them. The public image of negotiation as concession clashes with citizens' views of their leaders and representatives as strong for the right, courageous against odds, unshakable under fire, and not prone to cave in, sell out, give up, or be walked over. Public and press can enmesh a negotiator in a net of symbols, loyalties, obligations, and accountability procedures that keep his latitude limited. It is enough to drive any conscientious negotiator to secrecy.

Negotiators may themselves make statements to assuage or divert public opinion, as Harriman explained: "Now, there are plenty of things that we have to say for our domestic record, and it's always well to tell the other fellow, 'Don't pay too much attention to that, we have to say these things. You know they're not true, I'm saying them not for your benefit but for the home public. You know them already'" (Harriman interview). In fact, a major problem for a negotiator is to separate the noise from the message, a problem far more difficult and more complex than such a simple statement might suggest. Thus because the external context is heavy with noise, negotiators seek secrecy where they can concentrate on the message.

In an age of mass communications, a new and complicating factor in negotiations is that negotiators may seek to influence public opinion in other countries than their own. Many observers commented on President Sadat's skillful use of the mass media to publicize his positions in his negotiations with Israel in late 1977 and to reach out to audiences in the United States, the Middle East, and around the world; over the next three years one of his strategies was to educate the Israeli population to put pressure on its leaders from below, and he eventually helped defeat the Begin government at the polls. The mass media have become a tool of negotiations: a way of mobilizing support, of bringing pressure to bear that goes beyond those few people who have decision-making power, and also a way of limiting and shaping the options open to decision-makers (see Lewis, 1977).

The arguments against secrecy are no less correct. Secrecy is no refuge, since at some point the public will know anyhow. In an age of so-called sunshine laws, it may even have a right to know early in the process. Controlled information from a high government source may meet the requirements, but the major underlying argument about accountable and responsible government returns: as long as there is no way to verify what officials say, we cannot know whether the information is correct, so why should high officials play it straight?

In the end, what is important is the balance between the attainment of concrete results and the retention of abstract values. The fact is that there are few examples of a publicly negotiated solution of a difficult conflict. Even where open sessions are held—as in the United Nations—the real negotiations take place in the corridors or behind closed doors. Another fact is that delaying public disclosure of the process merely postpones the debate, often to a less favorable time. The delay in no way guarantees or even facilitates ratification. But the countervailing fact is that secrecy too often leads to abuse. Somewhere between "too much" and "too little" is an optimal working compromise, involving secret negotiations, participation of public representatives, and regular news accounts whenever possible.

HIGHER AND LOWER AND FRONT AND BACK CHANNELS

The relationship between the negotiator and the home front may be described in terms of channels. A high level channel can be most useful if it is not used to excess so as to undercut or replace the negotiator's role at the bargaining table. This study does not seek to deal comprehensively with the subject of summitry, that is, formal programmed discussions between heads of state, a subject that has been much discussed elsewhere. Suffice it to say here that conventional summitry is looked upon with considerable skepticism by most practicing negotiators because heads of state cannot be adequately familiar with all of the details of a complex negotiation. Summits, however, can be useful (1) in formalizing agreements previously hammered out by negotiating teams; and (2) in developing personal relationships between heads of state that may be utilized at critical points in future negotiations. These relationships may be referred to as back channels. If things get stuck up front, it sometimes takes the prestige and flexibility of a high level figure with an inside track to the head of state or government to start things moving again or to float a new approach that might be lost in the front channel. It is not always flattering to the working delegation up front, but sometimes it is necessary to restore momentum.

The letter from President Eisenhower that Robert Murphy carried in 1954 to President Tito of Yugoslavia appealing for his help in getting the logjam broken on the Trieste dispute is credited by Vladimir Velebit, the Yugoslav negotiator, with reopening communication (Campbell 1976, p. 103). Harriman also relates, in another incident from his experience, that an appeal from the president of the United States was the instrumental difference in reaching agreement on stabilizing the price of a commodity:

> I approached the talks [with Eduardo Frei, president of Chile] by explaining the difficulties our president had in the world, and his concern for maintaining the stability of the United States and avoiding inflation. But the important thing about this was that I simply said to him, "The President of the United States has sent me to see you and ask your help." He said, "You make it very difficult for me. There's nothing that is more difficult for me to do." The next day he asked me to come back. He said he had thought over our discussion and would accept a substantial compromise. This is a very important thing, to know when you can appeal to a man's better instincts. It was sobering for him to think that he, the president of rather a small country, had received such a request. (Harriman interview)

It may also be discouraging to the delegation not to be informed of higher level initiatives, but secrecy is sometimes necessary to break impasses. Front channels are also useful for totally different functions, notably as a public negotiating screen for more delicate private talks. The front channel may be the propaganda arm, covering up for concessions, or it may be the intelligence arm, sounding out the other side on its demands and flexibility in preparation for a direct offer through the back channel. A problem can arise, of course, when the front channel thinks it is negotiating rather than merely emitting propaganda or receiving intelligence.

Good examples of different uses of front and back channels are found in the SALT I and the Paris Vietnam negotiations. In the former, much work was done by the front channel, both in negotiation and intelligence, but the back was needed on occasion to break up logjams. In the latter, little work was done at the official negotiating sessions but they provided a screen of verbiage that the Vietnamese seemed to find useful and that, again, enabled each side to probe the other side's intentions. Sometimes one wonders whether such elaborate—and, after all, expensive—charades are necessary. The answer may well lie in requirements of the respective cultures; even the three years of Vietnam negotiations, with all their misunderstanding and hostility, seemed to require a semipublic forum as well as a secret substance in order to make progress. Something, no matter how hostile and outwardly unproductive, was necessary to symbolize continuity when the secret talks were on the rocks.

LONG AND SHORT REINS

The subject of diplomatic reins, also concerns the relationship between the head of state and the negotiator. Few diplomats—or at least few Western diplomats—like to be merely mouthpieces, unable to agree even on the next meeting date without a word from the home office. But there are occasions when the chief executive wants to hold a negotiator on a short rein. Averell Harriman recounted such an instance from his experience:

> During the war, I think one of the reasons why Roosevelt picked me was because he knew that I wouldn't give him any trouble. If he'd picked a member of his cabinet, it might be different. For instance, when I went to negotiate the supply agreement in 1941, both Morgenthau and Knox were anxious to go, but he picked me. I think one of the reasons why he picked me was because he knew that he could overrule me and it wouldn't be of any embarrassment to him, whereas if he overruled a member of his Cabinet, it would be difficult. (Harriman interview)

On the other hand, few diplomats like to have total

latitude and responsibility without some indication of the limits of acceptability for an agreement that will ultimately have to be sold to the many jealous executive agencies, if not to a suspicious legislature.

A negotiator may take steps to insure access to the top decision-maker. In his memoirs, Dean Acheson wrote about his role as backstop to General George Marshall during his mission to China:

> The General said that he would need what was known in the Army as a rear echelon, a person left behind with right of access at any time to the Commander-in-Chief, in this case, the President, through whom General Marshall could communicate. This man would bear personal responsibility for immediate reply and for action upon his requests, with authority to call on the President himself for help, if necessary to get action. The General would want an Army officer detailed to handle incoming and outgoing messages through Army channels, which would be used exclusively, as they were the only reliable facilities in China. The officer would deliver the messages to the rear echelon personally. . . . General Marshall wanted personal, not institutional, responsibility. He was no stranger to Washington bureaucracy.
>
> When the President agreed and asked whom he would select, the General said that he would like to have me charged with this duty. He asked that my assuming it be cleared with Secretary Byrnes, pointing out that I would necessarily have to act out of channels and probably annoy a good many people in fulfilling this assignment. My intuition was entirely correct. (Acheson 1969, pp. 143–44)

Somewhere in between, perhaps closer to the pole of independent responsibility, is the most comfortable position for a negotiator. But there are two sides to each pole. A

negotiator finds it convenient to float personal ideas informally, perhaps even as a basis for making recommendations
back home. A negotiator also finds it useful to be able to hide
behind the need to get new instructions from time to time. In
other words, as might be expected, latitude is useful in putting forth one's own ideas and constraint is useful in accepting the other's proposals.

Negotiators often find it useful to be able to say that they
are limited in their ability to compromise or in their margin
of flexibility by instructions from home. "Checking back" is
a way to indicate a negotiator's flexibility on a given issue
without necessarily conceding a point. To say one is limited
by instructions or that one does not have the authority to
commit something may or may not be true, but it is a way to
test the waters for the temperature of the other side's position without necessarily making any commitments. Secretary Dulles at one time discussed a possible security treaty in
Australia with the Australians and New Zealanders. In the
end it looked as if a treaty would make sense, but Dulles left
behind a letter that said, "I must emphasize that I have not
authority to commit my Government to its acceptance. . . . As
I told you the instructions of our mission contemplated a
Pacific security arrangement more comprehensive than
merely a Treaty between three countries" (Spender 1969, p.
159).

Other means to maintain flexibility in negotiations are
measures that break the formal rigidity of plenary sessions,
such as the use of subordinates, corridors, and tea breaks.
Whether at the point of searching for a formula or hunting
down a detail, occasions to sound out "what would happen
if . . ." on an informal or personal basis are usually helpful.
In fact, one would think that a good negotiating team would
be continually bombarding the other party with ideas, variations, innovations, thrusting and sparring to try to find the
limits of acceptability, the points of real disagreement, the

holes in defense, the thickness of the arguments of the other side. The corollary is that each party should avoid debates and battles lest he force the other to dig in on an undesirable position. The point is to loosen up the other party, make him think in new ways, press him to face those points in his position that he can yield without compromising the essentials. As long as they do not lead to undermining one's own position on the essentials, any techniques of informal discussion are helpful.

THE CULTURAL CONTEXT OF NEGOTIATIONS

The most troublesome question at the end of an inquiry of this type concerns the role of culture. Do people from different cultures have a different conception of the function of negotiation? Do they negotiate differently? Immediately this simple question dissolves into a number of definitional difficulties and problems of generalization. Any question dealing with national cultures brings with it the pitfalls of stereotypes partly anchored in reality and partly imaginary. Do Arabs negotiate like rug merchants, Africans palaver, and Orientals negotiate inscrutably? But then, is the relevant family "Arab" or Saudi, Moroccan, Egyptian, and so forth? Do all Africans negotiate like "Africans?" Are all Orientals equally inscrutable? It is easy to show the ridiculous stereotypes on which cultural generalizations are based, and yet there is something under it all which conforms to reality.

Many analysts have considered the cultural context in writing about specific negotiations. Dennett and Johnson, for example, put together a useful collection on negotiating with the Russians, Whelan skillfully analyzed a quarter-century of experience since then, and Kennan added his own observations on their idiosyncrasies. One of the main pitfalls in wartime and immediate postwar Anglo–American negotiations with the Soviet Union, in Philip Mosely's view, was the tendency of the United States and Great Britain to rely upon reaching an "agreement in principle" without spelling out in sufficient detail all the steps necessary for execution, since in his view the Russians did not share the same conception of principles or approaches to negotiations. Kennan (1951, p. 563) advised: "Do not encourage high-level exchanges of views with the Russians unless the initiative comes at least 50 percent from their side. Russians can be dealt with satisfactorily only when they themselves want something and feel themselves in a desperate position. It should be a matter of technique with us to see that they are not dealt with on a high level except when these conditions prevail." Clearly Kennan's conclusions were based in part upon his view of structural differences between the United States amd the Soviet Union but also apparently upon his view of Russian character. Lloyd Jensen (1978) used mathematical techniques to demonstrate that Russians concede late and Americans concede early, as a behavioral pattern. The Kennedys specifically set out to reverse this pattern in the Cuban missile crisis, as already noted.

Sir Harold Nicolson's useful typologies of what he called Shopkeeper and Warrior were drawn from his views of the English (a nation of shopkeepers) and Germans (a nation of militarists). He portrayed the English as non-zero-sum negotiators and the Germans as zero-sum negotiators. Mushakoji (1972) and Blaker (1977) compared Japanese and Western cultural differences and their effects on negotiation. Zartman (1971) noted that the East Africans, in negotiating, followed a cultural rule of "talking until they agree," on the assumption that talk necessarily arrives at consensus—but the West Africans showed no such "African" proclivities. Bozeman (1976) has found evidence that Africans of different cultures do have basically different negotiating patterns.

It has been noted that perceptions are functionally selective and that no one perceives every aspect of a situation or a relationship. Even "facts" may be perceived in quite different ways. Careful negotiators seek to develop a shared definition of the situation. Cultural differences lead individuals to bring different sets of assumptions to the bargaining situation, and it may be important to make these differences overt.

Culture then does affect the perceptions and assumptions of negotiators, yet two equally valid counterarguments can be made. One is that negotiation is a universal process, utilizing a finite number of behavioral patterns, and that cultural differences are simply differences in style and language—much as one could say that there are a limited number of basic game patterns and the differences between basketball and hockey are variations, albeit important, on a basic theme. The other argument, on an entirely different level, is that by now the world has established an international diplomatic culture that soon socializes its members into similar behavior. Even the Chinese have learned to play the U.N. game by its rules, newly independent countries such as the African nations attach themselves to their former colonial delegations for general advice until they have learned the ropes, and groups of delegates teach the newer members about diplomatic ways originally developed for a European state system. It is difficult to maintain, as Nicolson and Morgenthau did, that the Western system of diplomacy and negotiation worked out over the centuries is in danger of imminent destruction at the hands of people who cannot comprehend our ways; to the contrary, the new nations have learned the Western ways well and are using them to their own purposes.

It is difficult to conclude—from the series of interviews with a multinational sample of U.N. ambassadors designed to determine this very matter—that there are dominant cultural influences on negotiations. In the interviews referred to in chapter 1 an attempt was made to measure the possible impact on negotiations of the cultural factor. Slightly fewer than half of the ambassadors responded that approaches to negotiations were determined by factors other than culture. Of the 55 percent of negotiators who answered the second question classifying five national groups—Arab, Latin American, Chinese, Soviet, European—according to differences in their bargaining approaches, half responded that all of the groups adopted a "tough" concession approach. If all of these groups were classified as tough negotiators by those who felt that culture does play a role, then the distinctive role it plays is hard to ferret out.

All of the arguments, pro and con, are valid. Where do they meet, to indicate the role of culture in negotiation? How can cultural behavior be used or neutralized? A few guidelines seem evident. First, there is no cultural exclusiveness. If Qaddafi and Mintoff seem to be good examples of "Mediterranean cliffhangers," not using minimax rationality, starting wild, conceding little, and raising demands during negotiations, not all such negotiating behavior is Mediterranean nor do all Mediterraneans act in this way.

Second, there is a whole cultural area that is real but only peripheral to the understanding of the basic negotiating process, and this relates to language, cultural connotations, social rules and taboos, and other aspects of communication. One study suggests that cultural static between two groups who do not understand each other's rules for communication can become so high as to keep messages from reaching their destination at all, causing the negotiations to break down (Spector 1976, pp. 366–70). In the Vietnam Paris negotiations, cultural static exacerbated by ideological predispositions made communications—and underlying it all, trust—extremely difficult. Important as this is, however, it does not change the basic nature of the process or the applicability of the discussion in earlier chapters.

Third, within the framework of the preceding discussion, there are national differences in negotiating behavior. They exist at several levels. Most simply, the difference that has been accentuated in this review—between "inductive" or detail-type and "deductive" or formula-type negotiation—is often reflected in national behavior. Many SALT negotiators have suggested that Russians prefer to work on the level of details, that is, they start high and proceed by concessions, whereas Americans look for a formula from which the agreeable details will flow. It can further be suggested that these differences refer not simply to some circular cultural definition but more deeply to the nature of negotiation in the respective political systems. Because Americans negotiate as publicly as possible, high openers followed by concessions would be subjected to debate in the media and probably to criticism for "giving in." The Russian *kto-kogo* ("Who will bury whom?") ideology of confrontation is more compatible with concession/convergence bargaining than formula negotiation; as long as negotiations are secret—a point the Russians frequently insist on with vehemence—there is little danger of exposure of concession-making and in any case there is little public before which the issue can be debated.

On another level, cultural differences stem from the variegated components of national value structures. Several scholars, including Druckman and others (1977) in an important review of past work and a report on additional experiments, showed strong variations by national ("cultural") group on such matters as competitiveness, time it takes to reach agreement, and compromise/convergence. But they also showed that these behaviors were related to underlying values, notably different views of justice (partial, impartial, equity, redistribution, as discussed in chapter 2). An Asian approach to negotiations, for example, is often termed elastic (Mushakoji 1972). Asian negotiators are accustomed to living with greater diversities than are representatives from many other cultures and thus feel at ease resolving the specifics of a particular dispute without necessarily agreeing to everything an adversary calls for. Thus they are more easily able to agree to disagree.

Some of these behavioral "symptoms" a negotiator can learn to deal with, or at least expect. (Communist countries like Russia and China seem to like to negotiate late at night, although Marx and Lenin were not very explicit on this particular subject.) The deeper "causes," the value structures, may be more difficult to handle, particularly if they cover antithetical notions of justice. Behind the maverick behavior of Mintoff and Qaddafi was a redistributive notion of justice that prevented much agreement on a formula. In other cases, however, it is helpful to know the opponent's definition of justice and try to design a formula for a solution to fit those terms, if possible. The important point is, however, that these idiosyncratic differences can be interpreted within the framework of the process as it has been discussed above: it is still better to find a formula, it is still necessary to define details, and within those needs it is still important to communicate to the other party in signals that he understands.

Appendix: Interviews

Complete transcripts of the interviews conducted for the Communication and Conflict Program of the Academy for Educational Development, are part of the Oral History Collection of Columbia University. Identifications are those current when interviews were conducted.

Philip C. Jessup, former Ambassador at Large

Robert A. Lovett, former Under Secretary of State and Secretary of Defense

Theodore W. Kheel, labor mediator

John J. McCloy, former High Commissioner for Germany

George C. McGhee, former Ambassador to Turkey and to the Federal Republic of Germany and Under Secretary of State for Political Affairs

Livingston T. Merchant, former Ambassador to Canada and Under Secretary of State for Political Affairs

Robert T. Murphy, former Ambassador to Belgium and to Japan and Under Secretary of State

Kenneth Rush, Ambassador to France

J. Robert Schaetzel, former Ambassador to the European Communities

Phillips Talbot, former Ambassador to Greece and Assistant Secretary of State for Near Eastern and South Asian Affairs

Llewellyn Thompson, former Ambassador to the Soviet Union

Charles W. Yost, former Permanent Representative to the United Nations

Non-Americans

Frederick S. Arkhurst (Ghana), former Ambassador and negotiator representing the African Economic Commission

Manlio Brosio (Italy), former Ambassador to the Soviet Union and to Great Britain and Secretary-General of NATO

Lord Caradon (Great Britain), former Permanent Representative to the United Nations

Rajeshwar Dayal (India), former Permanent Representative to the United Nations

Geoffrey W. Harrison (Great Britain), former Ambassador to Brazil, to Iran, and to the Soviet Union

Max Jakobson (Finland), former Permanent Representative to the United Nations

Khwaja Kaiser (Bangladesh), Permanent Representative to the United Nations

Dirk Spierenburg (Netherlands), former Permanent Representative to the European Economic Community and Permanent Representative to NATO

Ernst van der Beugel (Netherlands), Representative to the European Economic Community

Index

245